PHOTOSH FOR INTERIOR DESIGNERS

A Nonverbal Communication

FAIRCHILD BOOKS
Bloomsbury Publishing Inc
1385 Broadway, New York, NY 10018, USA
50 Bedford Square, London, WC1B 3DP, UK

BLOOMSBURY, FAIRCHILD BOOKS and the Fairchild Books logo are trademarks of Bloomsbury Publishing Plc

First published in the United States of America 2014
Reprinted 2019, 2020 (twice)

For legal purposes the Acknowledgments on p. ix constitute an extension of this copyright page.

Cover Design: Carly Grafstein
Cover Art Credit: Suining Ding
Layout Design by Loretta Reilly Design, Inc.

A catalog record for this book is available from the Library of Congress
2013935322

ISBN: PB: 978-1-60901-544-2
ePDF: 978-1-60901-855-9
ePUB: 978-1-60901-056-3

Typeset by Precision Graphics
Printed and bound in Great Britain

To find out more about our authors and books visit www.fairchildbooks.com and sign up for our newsletter.

PHOTOSHOP® FOR INTERIOR DESIGNERS
A Nonverbal Communication

SUINING DING, ASID, IDEC

INDIANA UNIVERSITY–PURDUE UNIVERSITY INDIANAPOLIS

FAIRCHILD BOOKS

NEW YORK · LONDON · OXFORD · NEW DELHI · SYDNEY

Contents

Chapter Six: Special Effects in Photoshop

Chapter Seven: Adding Entourage

Chapter Eight: Working with Freehand Drawings

Chapter Nine: Composing Drawings with InDesign

Chapter Ten: Creating Presentation Drawings Using Multiple Software Programs

Preface

Unique Features of the Book

A good designer has to have good presentation skills that enable him or her to communicate a design concept quickly and professionally. I have taught interior design studio courses for many years, and I always found it challenging even for senior students to present their design concepts visually in a quick and speedy manner. After years of teaching and exploration, I have found that using several different software products to create presentation boards is an efficient method. Using an approach that integrates Adobe Photoshop, Autodesk AutoCAD, Trimble SketchUp, and freehand drawings as well as Adobe InDesign to compose drawings and prepare presentation boards is invaluable in today's world of design. This approach allows the designer to enhance the drawings to create a professional and polished finished project. Although the focus of the book is on the use of Photoshop to enhance 3D models, the book also shows how to use SketchUp and lay out the presentation boards with InDesign.

A good designer should have excellent communication skills, including verbal, written, and visual skills. In this book, the emphasis is on visual communication that combines graphic images and explanatory text. This book is a case in point, using written and visual communication to express ideas.

A unique feature of this book that distinguishes it from others is that, instead of focusing on a single specific computer program, it uses Photoshop, SketchUp, and InDesign to compose drawings and prepare presentation boards. Each software program has specialized functions in which it excels. Using them in combination ensures the most polished final product made in the most quick and efficient manner.

Another unique feature is that demonstrations and sample drawings are used as a thread throughout the book. Although Photoshop has been used widely for graphics, combining Photoshop with SketchUp and freehand drawing is relatively new to the design field. I am an advocate of using freehand sketching in schematic designs even in this digital era. I believe that freehand line expresses a uniquely individual human thought process and action in the early schematic design phase that cannot be expressed digitally. People recognize the human attributes and personality in freehand lines, marks, and strokes, even with slight imperfections. Combining digital media and freehand drawing provides more flexibility and brings a unique quality of graphic communication to the schematic design phase.

Prerequisite Knowledge for the Book and Versions of Software

This book targets an audience that does not have much previous experience using Photoshop, SketchUp, and InDesign. Step-by-step demonstrations that are easy to follow for beginning level learners are provided.

The book is presented in a generic manner that allows it to be used with both older and newer versions of the software. The book also strives to use basic commands and functions of the programs, because these do not change much from version to version.

The current new version of Photoshop is CS6. The first thing you notice about Photoshop CS6 is its new interface. You now have the choice between four base colors, from near-black to pale gray. Everything has been subtly tweaked, from the hundreds of redesigned icons (the Pen and Lasso tools now indicate their active hotspots more clearly) to a crisper, more consistent layout. Other subtly tweaked features include filters, lighting effects filters, and layers. However, all these differences do not affect the procedures or tool icons.

Pedagogical Framework of the Textbook

Chapters in the book have pedagogical features that are designed to assist teaching and enhance learning. Demonstrations are an important feature of this book. To help explain and demonstrate the concepts and techniques, the book includes detailed examples. Each chapter begins with a brief introduction, which is followed by demonstrations and exercises. Each chapter then ends with a summary, a list of key terms, and additional exercises. Many drawings are included to provide inspirations for students.

During my years teaching studio courses and teaching software, I found that learning-by-doing and project-based learning approaches increase students' enthusiasm and accelerate the learning progress. Once a solid foundation of basic concepts and skills is mastered, the student can progress naturally to the next level.

Comprehensive Supplements

To support the study of *Photoshop® for Interior Designers*, the text is accompanied by the following supplement for the instructor:

- Instructor's Guide

    - Chapter outlines with suggestions for lectures, discussion, and additional projects

    - Teaching tips for mobile devices, collaborative activities, case studies, and maximizing student learning

    - Sample course outlines

And for the student:

- Companion website with editable design templates to use for the projects at the end of chapters

Organization of the Textbook

Because of the importance of visual presentation skills in the interior design curriculum and profession, this book is written for college-level studio courses or presentation technique courses as well as for design professionals who want to reinforce their presentation skills using multiple software programs. It provides readers with more systematic demonstrations and exercise. The text is organized to enable an instructor to teach the visual communication principles as a foundation for composing the presentation drawings, and then gradually move from very basic techniques to the next level.

The textbook is sequentially written and organized to develop the skills from visual communication principles, the fundamentals of Photoshop, as well as the special features of Photoshop, Trimble SketchUp, and InDesign. The book is organized into ten chapters, as follows.

Chapter One: Visual Communications and Photoshop Fundamentals, orients students with visual communication principles including organizing for visual perception, guiding the visual process, clarifying for visual complexity, and expressing visual meanings. It then introduces the fundamentals of Photoshop. In this chapter, several examples of presentation drawings are given, which will ultimately lead readers to Chapter 10, which introduces a detailed drawing composing process using InDesign.

Chapter Two: Working with Floor Plans and Elevations, demonstrates creating both floor plan and interior elevations with Photoshop. In addition to basic techniques and tools, how to bring photographed materials and textures to drawings is demonstrated. The techniques also include how to add photos and entourages, such as human figures, plants, and cars, to drawings.

Chapter Three: Working with Perspectives and Isometric Views, introduces techniques of creating and enhancing both perspectives and isometric drawings with Photoshop. A rough 3D model is created in SketchUp and then enhanced in Photoshop. The techniques of using Photoshop to enhance and refine perspective and isometric views include bringing in framed pictures, creating drop shadows, creating shadows on the floor, adding human figures, adding lighting effects, creating exterior views in perspective, and bringing furniture to perspective drawing.

Chapter Four: Working with Materials, introduces the techniques of applying materials in Photoshop to enhance and refine the perspective. It shows how a rough 3D model can be created in SketchUp and saved in PDF format. Then the drawings are enhanced in Photoshop by adding materials to the floor, walls, and ceiling.

Chapter Five: Working with Lighting, introduces basic techniques of applying lighting to perspective drawings. It starts with the preexisting lighting types in the Photoshop system. Then more advanced techniques are demonstrated through tutorials. Tutorials featured include applying mixed lighting in interior space, creating cast shadows for the objects, and creating cast lighting for stained glass windows. In addition, creating floor reflections is described. Through the tutorials, techniques of lighting and shadow are demonstrated, including manually adding lighting and shadow.

Chapter Six: Special Effects in Photoshop, introduces techniques of creating special effects by using various Photoshop filters. The special effects include creating sepia and sepia with pastel color in order to give the presentation an old-time or vintage look and adding watercolor and pastel effects to impart a looser, hand-drawn look.

Chapter Seven: Adding Entourage, demonstrates how to add entourage such as people, plants, and cars to drawings. The chapter also demonstrates how to create shadows for entourages, and especially how to create a shadow on a vertical wall.

Chapter Eight: Working with Freehand Drawings, introduces techniques of transforming freehand drawings to digital drawings in Photoshop. Adding photographed materials and entourage to digital drawings is also demonstrated, as well as further exploration of adding watercolor effects.

Chapter Nine: Composing Drawings with InDesign, introduces the fundamentals of InDesign and demonstrates how to compose a poster in InDesign. All individual drawings are first prepared in Photoshop. Then how to add text to the poster in InDesign is covered. A case study of a visual narrative of the Pantheon is included as well.

Chapter Ten: Creating Presentation Drawings Using Multiple Software Programs introduces techniques of using various software programs to compose posters. Although the emphasis is on SketchUp, creating posters using AutoCAD, Photoshop, and InDesign is also described. The ultimate goal of using multiple programs to create professional-looking and high-quality posters in an efficient way is stressed throughout the tutorials.

Editable digital files for students to use to complete the projects at the end of chapters are on the book's companion website located at http://www.bloomsbury.com/us/photoshop-for-interior-designers-9781609015442/.

It is my privilege to introduce this approach of creating presentation drawings. It is also my goal to introduce techniques that can be used to create presentation drawings quickly and easily. I hope that the pedagogical approach in this book will help you to become a better designer who is able to use multiple digital media to compose drawings and prepare presentation boards. I strongly believe that visual communication skills are as important as verbal and written communication skills, especially for talented and creative designers.

Suining Ding, ASID, IDEC

Acknowledgments

I have many individuals to thank for their help with this book. First and foremost, I extend my heartfelt thank-you to Olga Kontzias, executive editor, a dedicated interior design education supporter, and an accomplished and skilled editor. The evolution of the book was driven by inspirational conversations with her. Olga not only saw value in this book but also was personally involved with every aspect of this book's organization. I am grateful for the team support and efforts provided by Fairchild Books. I extend my heartfelt thanks to my experienced team of editors: Joseph Miranda, senior development editor, for his encouragement, help, and collaboration in the development process. I also extend my gratitude to production editor Jessica Katz for her help and thoroughness in the editing process. It has always been a great experience working with such skillful and professional editors. I appreciate their collegial collaborations in the process of accomplishing a nicely finished book. I am also grateful for the review and constructive criticism of proposal reviewers and manuscript development reviewers, which include Gayla Jett Shannon, Texas Christian University; Charlene B. Reed, Orange Coast College; Lindsay Tan, Auburn University; Sheila Flener, Western Kentucky University; Hans-Christian Lischewski, Mount Ida College; and Kathleen Ryan, Washington State University.

I wish to thank my students, who made this manuscript possible by contributing AutoCAD line drawings and allowing me to use these drawings in Photoshop. My warmest thanks go to Megan Bobay, Alexis Dancer, and Jade Rice.

I am deeply grateful to my family and friends, who remained loyal and supportive while I was away from their life and spent hours and hours writing and creating drawings. I would not have been able to write this book without the unconditional support from my family and dear friends. I am grateful to my parents, who have always been the inspirations for my scholarly endeavor.

Visual Communications and Photoshop Fundamentals

Interior designers and architects must be able to communicate their design concepts visually through graphics in the design process particularly in the schematic design phase. Presentation drawings serve as a vital aid for designers in the design process to help clients envision the proposed work. The drawings that designers prepare for their clients should tell the story without the designers necessarily being present to explain the drawings. That means the components in drawings must convey meanings in a very strong visual language.

This book introduces unique methods for providing cognitive meaning through visual language. The book uses Photoshop to inspire new and creative ways of visual communication for interior designers. This first chapter describes principles of creating visual images in interior design and architectural drawings that are comprehensive, memorable, and informative.

Visual Language in Design

Imagery enables viewers to comprehend concepts that are difficult to explain through words. Using basic design components, the designer can bypass some of the difficulties of conveying meanings through verbal language. For example, an interior perspective drawing can convey the spatial relationships of a building. In fact, designers would have great difficulty talking about the spatial relationship in verbal terms without any drawings, such as floor plans, elevations, sections, and perspectives. These drawings are basic components in a drawing or presentation board.

But how does the designer approach composing all these basic drawings and conveying design concepts? This book introduces a simple, quick, and creative way to accomplish this goal: using Adobe's Photoshop software package to enhance images and make them more dynamic.

As mentioned in the Preface, the unique approach of this book is to use various software packages to present a visual narrative. For example, the designer could use SketchUp or 3D AutoCAD to generate a rough raw model, then use Photoshop to enhance the model by adding lighting and materials, and. finally, use InDesign to compose the presentation boards. Or the designer could use other modeling programs such as 3D Studio Max (now Autodesk 3ds Max, though commonly referred to by its former name) or Revit to create rough raw models, and then use Photoshop to refine the 3D models quickly and easily to create professional-looking and more realistic 3D models. Each software package has its own unique features. Photoshop is a powerful tool that allows the designer to enhance images by adding or changing materials, texture, color, and other image attributes—and it is the common thread and focus of this book. However, Photoshop is not a 3D modeling software program like 3D AutoCAD, 3D Studio, or Revit. SketchUp is a free software program that is easy to use, but the generated models do not look as realistic as models generated by its pricier counterparts—3DAutoCAD, 3D Studio Max, or Revit. Yet the models generated by SketchUp can be easily enhanced with Photoshop to add realistic materials and true-to-life lighting effects. In this way, using Photoshop with modeling programs can save time and budget.

Photoshop is also not a page-layout program. InDesign, the design package offered as part of Adobe's Creative Suite with Photoshop, is tailored specifically for page layout or creating presentation boards. It provides more flexibility than Photoshop for page layout. This is where using a variety of programs is logical and efficient.

A multi-software approach also frees up one of the designer's most cherished commodities: time. The designer doesn't need to spend a lot of time generating 3D models, a more mechanical part of the job. This allows the designer to do what he or she does best—designing.

Visual Communication Principles

In order to create meaningful presentation drawings that are informative, unique, aesthetically pleasing, and able to captivate the human mind and emotions, designers must understand visual communication principles. These principles are guides rather than rules, and they are intended to serve as a catalyst for finding visual solutions and fine-tuning one's work.

Drawings serve as the common language among designers. Presentation drawings and boards or posters also serve as visual language to convey design intent to clients. A professional presentation board should not only describe the spatial relationship of the building but also convey the design concept and meanings—what the designer intends to express. Visual communication is also fitting for today's multilingual, global culture. György Kepes, an art educator and influential designer, said that "visual communication is universal and international; it knows no limits of tongue, vocabulary, or grammar, and it can be perceived by the illiterate as well as by the literate." Therefore, presentation drawings must be meaningful and must represent the story of the project concept and history. They should also represent the designer's intent in a way that viewers can understand.

The Meaning of Presentation Drawings

A drawing is more than a two-dimensional, marked surface. It presents the creator's intent and indicates that there is a great deal of information to be communicated. It is the manifestation of creative ideas and thoughtful decisions meant to evoke an emotional visual experience. Designers create drawings and graphics with the assumption that viewers will understand their message by viewing line, color, and shape—and that a communication will be transmitted. Designers also assume the viewer will proceed through a graphic in an orderly sequence, controlled by the designer's expression of visual elements and hierarchy.

Therefore, the designer must evaluate the work from the viewer's perspective. Can the viewer understand the designer's concept and intention presented in a visual image? How can the designer ensure that the audience will understand and interpret the intention completely and correctly? Viewers perceive drawings differently depending on their preconceived ideas and values. Studies indicate that age, gender, educational background, culture, and language are other aspects that influence perception (Malamed, 2009, p. 20). Furthermore, trained artists would perceive and interpret visual images differently than non-artists because of different foci in the visual perception process. Trained artists usually spend more time looking at the background and the relationships among elements, such as color, light, shape, and spatial relationship, while non-artists usually spend more time looking at central objects. Therefore, the visual perception process is very complicated and the designer cannot fully anticipate what the viewers would interpret and perceive from visual images.

It is paramount to understand the nature of the human visual perception process in order to help the designer in the drawing creation process. The following visual communication principles provide guidance to designers while they are creating their drawings or visual narratives. (Malamed, 2009, p. 20).

Principle 1:
Organize for Visual Perception

Organizing for visual perception comprises four major components: focal point, pop-out focal point, visible texture segregation, and grouping visual elements. Understanding these four components and how to organize them in images will help designers create drawings that can be interpreted and perceived by viewers correctly and effectively (Malamed, 2009, p. 47).

Focal Point

The focal point includes primary objects that will catch viewers' eyes immediately when they look at an image. The designer can control the focal point by using different color, orientation, and size in order to distinguish it from other objects in the background. The designer wants to draw viewers' attention to a certain key focal point of the designed space to inform the design direction.

Pop-Out Focal Point

Studies show that before consciously paying attention, viewers rapidly analyze graphics and register the features that **pop out** (Malamed, 2009, p. 54). Viewers scan the entire graphic image quickly before paying more attention to a specific object. As designers, we want viewers to pay conscious attention to the focal point. To achieve this goal, designers must ensure a strong contrast is made between a focal point object and the background and non–focal point objects. This is achieved through color (e.g., using complementary colors), texture (e.g., smooth versus rough), and value (e.g., dark against light).

Figure 1.1 illustrates making a **primitive feature** pop out. This figure presents a design concept for a commercial space inside a historic building. The design intent is to create a space with a modern twist that is inviting and appealing and also conveys an undertone of simplicity and elegance. In order to draw viewers' eyes to the two interior perspectives, the color orange is applied to the furniture, which contrasts with the black-and-white scheme. When viewers look at this presentation drawing, their attention will be immediately drawn to the two interior perspectives, which present the new design solutions. The black-and-white photo of the building's exterior and city skyline tells the story about the historical building in a modern city where this newly designed commercial space will be located. All the components in this presentation drawing come together to convey the meaning through visual images.

Visible Texture Segregation

Through **texture segregation**, which means using different textures to distinguish different areas, we also can separate foreground from background. Typically, the area with texture catches the viewer's attention more quickly than the area without the texture. However, if an interior design perspective drawing is placed on a busy background with texture, the interior design perspective drawing with the texture would lose its pop-out effect. In other words, the interior design perspective would not become the focal point. The designer needs to make texture segregation visible so that viewers can understand the meaning of the presentation drawing and pay conscious attention to the focal point.

Figures 1.2 and 1.3 are examples of using different texture segregations to distinguish the images and the background. Figure 1.2 presents an Arts and Crafts–inspired design. Three perspective drawings are contrasted by two different textures. One is a smooth, gray-colored background, and the other is an exterior view of an Arts and Crafts building that has been blurred by the Photoshop Filter function. These three perspective drawings are enhanced with hand-rendered sepia tone color in Photoshop. (Making sepia drawings is introduced in Chapter 6.) The statement of this presentation drawing is to design a better building that will sustain the natural landscape by using Arts and Crafts design principles.

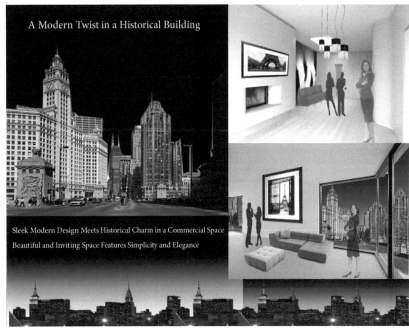

Figure 1.1

Figure 1.2

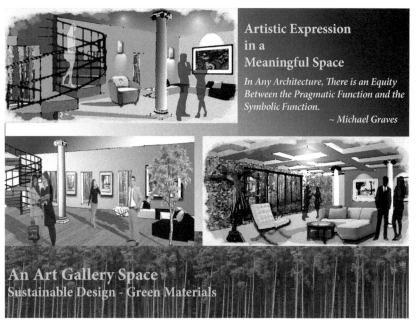

Figure 1.3

and interior perspective are the major components that display the spatial relationship as well as the style of the interior design. When viewers look at this presentation drawing, their attention should be drawn to these components. The tree background of the drawing and green color on all floor plans and section emphasize the story that the loft is in a natural setting and is designed as a green, sustainable building.

Principle 2:
Guide the Visual Process

As designers, we should not allow viewers to wander around the image without leading them through the visual process. A designer should assist viewers by guiding viewers' eyes through a well-composed drawing. As mentioned earlier, the focal point is the area that draws the viewer's attention and lets the viewer spend more time on reading and seeing. Therefore, the designer should lead viewers to the focal point immediately when the viewer first scans the images. The focal point could be the largest object in an image or the one with bright color, or it could be emphasized by strong contrast or texture. These "eye catchers" will cause the viewers to pause and spend time to extract information from the focal point.

Figures 1.1 and 1.2 demonstrate making a focal point pop out to guide viewers' eyes in comprehending designers' intentions. In both figures, interior perspectives are the focal points of the presentation drawings.

Position and Emphasis of Visual Elements

In order to lead viewers' visual processes, designers need to position the objects with different degrees of emphasis. Through careful arrangement of visual elements, designers should be able to establish a visual hierarchy to guide viewers.

Studies show that objects placed on the top half of a drawing are considered to be more active and draw viewers' attention easier than other positions. Another study found that viewers spend more time looking at objects appearing on the left and upper half of the drawing than objects located on the right and lower half. Therefore, it is important to consider these two aspects when composing a drawing.

Having various emphases in a drawing is key to creating a successful drawing. Different levels of emphasis will make your drawing more interesting and attractive. As mentioned earlier, emphasis can be achieved by creating contrast. Focal point is another method mentioned. Keep in mind that there should only be one focal point in a drawing. Figure 1.5 is an example of creating contrast by using different colors and creating emphasis to lead viewers' attention. In this presentation drawing, the main purpose is to make a statement that architecture

Figure 1.3 presents a gallery space design. Three perspective drawings are contrasted by two different textures. Since two perspective drawings are watercolor effect, they both are contrasted by a flat, gray-colored background. On the other hand, the green-tree background at the bottom of the drawing contrasts with the two perspective drawings because the texture of the background is different from the drawing texture. This causes the three perspective drawings to pop out and draw in the viewer's attention. The statement of this presentation drawing is to create a meaningful space that will be constructed by green materials. It will be a space that not only has function but also has a meaning that designers and artists want to express through their work, which in this case is to design a sustainable space.

Grouping Visual Elements

The perceptual organization of individual objects into a whole is based on the theories promoted by the Gestalt psychologists in the early twentieth century (Malamed, 2009, p. 66). The theories suggest that the human eye sees objects in their entirety before perceiving the individual parts. Viewers perceive elements that have similar visual characteristics, such as shape and texture, as one unit or one cluster. Therefore, according to Gestalt theory, a visual image that arranges elements into a group unit influences how viewers interpret and understand the images (Malamed, 2009). **Grouping visual elements** enhances the composition of the visual image because viewers know that clustered elements are in a similar category.

Figure 1.4 is an example of grouping visual elements. Three floor plans are grouped together; this takes precedence over the viewer seeing the individual parts. In this presentation drawing, the floor plans, building section,

is frozen music and that it is also a form of art that features rhythm, harmony, and order. The modern interior space in this presentation drawing is inspired by a classical interior space that features rhythm, harmony, and order. Classical column orders are used repetitively in a modern space so that rhythm and harmony are achieved. The piano and violin provide a reference to music that both implies and emphasizes the statement. In this presentation drawing, interior space is presented in black and white, while the piano and violin are shown in color. Therefore, the statement of architecture as frozen music is emphasized again by the color contrast.

Visual Cues—Color Cues

Color is an important design element that many designers like to use in their designs and drawings. Color conveys meanings and causes different interpretations because of the complicated visual process. Different people with different cultural backgrounds will have different perceptions of colors. In a color drawing, viewers will be drawn to the **color cues**. To ensure immediate attention from viewers, designers should use a different color on the focal point object so that it contrasts with the background or surrounding objects.

In Figure 1.1, a color cue is used to make two interior perspectives pop out and draw viewers' attention. In Figure 1.3, the color cue is used to emphasize the design intention of green design. In both presentation drawings, color cues serve as a vehicle to facilitate the interpretation and comprehension of visual information.

Principle 3:
Clarify for Visual Complexity

There are pros and cons associated with visual complexity. On the one hand, visual complexity captures viewers' attention and bears more interest for viewers. Viewers will tend to spend more time looking at objects with more details and diverse patterns. On the other hand, complexity can cause confusion or might lead viewers to avoid the image if it is extremely complex (Malamed, 2009). The designer must balance simplicity and complexity in order to attract viewers and let them pause and spend time reading the visual image.

Explanation of Complex Design Concepts

Interior design or architectural drawings include floor plans, elevations, sections, details, isometric views, perspectives, as well as other visual elements. These components are presented by using details, text, color, and pattern that convey meanings. Usually viewers will have an easier time understanding simpler drawings.

The approach is to clarify the complexity in drawings by revealing the components that are concealed. This can include creating a variety of interior design views, such

as cross sections and isometric views, as well as other details. This approach not only uncovers building system and details, but it also presents the spatial relationship of the space and how buildings are structured. Therefore, including sections, isometric views and details in drawings is an important strategy for complex drawings.

Figure 1.4 is an example of using a building section to explain complex content in order to reveal the spatial relationship of the building.

Figure 1.4

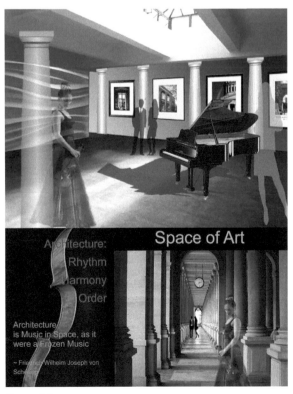

Figure 1.5

Principle 4: Express Visual Meanings

Interior design and architectural drawings must tell the story of the design concept and design process through visual elements. A good presentation drawing should convey meanings and tell the story by visual images without the designer being present. A written visual narrative should be presented by drawings that convey meanings.

Visual Narratives

The **visual narrative** form also transmits emotion. Narratives are a cognitively and emotionally natural way for people to communicate; humans are a species of storytellers. Telling a story combining visual images with a coherent theme draws viewers to the message. Narratives allow designers to create an underlying emotional track that runs through the visuals. Figures 1.1, 1.4, and 1.5 provide a narrative for each of the presentation drawings. Each narrative tells a story about the design and design concept.

There are many ways to present visual narratives. In the interior design and architectural design fields, poster presentation drawings are usually used, combining images and a short paragraph of text. In this digital era, sophisticated software is used extensively. In order to create a presentation drawing in a speedy way, a multi-software approach is used in this book, with an emphasis on Photoshop. The following starts with Photoshop fundamentals. Then more in-depth Photoshop applications will be discussed.

Photoshop Fundamentals

All of the presentation drawings in this book were created either in Photoshop or in InDesign. Some designers like to use Photoshop to compose presentation drawings, while others like to use InDesign. It is a personal preference and depends on the complexity and the size of the drawing. Photoshop can be used to edit drawings and photos, while InDesign can be used for composing presentation drawings, such as Figures 1.1, 1.3, 1.4, and 1.5. In presentation drawings or on a presentation board, the visual components include floor plans, sections, perspectives, isometric views, as well as details. The visual components can be created by AutoCAD, freehand sketching, Trimble SketchUp, and other software for a preliminary drawing. Then the designer can use Photoshop to edit and refine his or her drawings.

This book provides a step-by-step guide that will lead you from the preliminary drawing to a fine-tuned, finished presentation drawing using Photoshop. The goal is to introduce an easy, quick way to prepare professional presentation drawings that can convey a design concept for the viewer to interpret.

Following are the basic Photoshop functions designers can use for their drawings:

- Gradient fill, which can be used for floor plans, elevations, and sections as well as perspectives
- Materials application, which allows you to add real-looking materials in your drawings
- Lighting application, which allows you to simulate different types of lighting sources
- Filter gallery, which allows you to enhance your drawing with different special effects, such as watercolor, oil, pastel, and many others
- Import, which allows you to add human figures and landscaping from different drawings

These are just some of the major functions available in Photoshop. There are many other functions that designers can use, such as layer mask, clone stamp, and image adjustment. The following Photoshop functions are fundamentals that every designer should know before using this program for their drawings.

Brightness and Contrast

Brightness/Contrast image adjustment is a very handy and easy-to-use function in Photoshop. As the name indicates, this allows you to adjust your image's brightness and contrast. Designers might use this feature to reduce the contrast and increase the brightness of an image to use it for a background. To use image Brightness and Contrast adjustment, go to the Image pull-down menu on the toolbar. Then select Adjustment—Brightness/Contrast.

Image > Adjustment > Brightness/Contrast

Follow the prompts from the dialogue box as shown in Figure 1.6. Adjust the values in the dialogue box to change the brightness and contrast of the image. (Note that the image in Figure 1.6 is darker and has more contrast than the image in Figure 1.7.)

Black and White Adjustment

Sometimes you need a black-and-white drawing or photo as background for your presentation board. In Photoshop, changing a color drawing to black and white is easy. From the Image menu, select Adjustment—Black & White.

Image > Adjustment > Black & White...

The dialogue box shown in Figure 1.8 appears. Use the slider setting to adjust the proportion of the color components used to create a black-and-white conversion. Figure 1.9 shows the original color image.

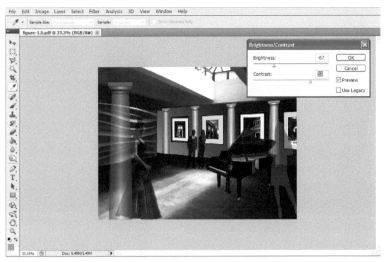

Figure 1.6

Figure 1.7

Figure 1.8

Figure 1.9

Photoshop Tools Panel

On the left side of your screen is a **Tools panel**. Many of the tools listed in the menu for this panel have a triangle in the bottom right corner of the tool icon, indicating that there are extra tools nested in a tool group. Placing your cursor on the tool icon reveals the list of tools shown in Figure 1.10.

Figure 1.11a–x illustrates all the tools in the Tools palette.

Shown in Figure 1.12, the toolbar at the top of the screen allows you to open files, manage layers, use the Change Image mode, find the Filter Gallery, and perform many other Photoshop functions. Detailed information on each of these tools and functions is given in subsequent chapters.

Figure 1.10

Tools Palette

Move tool (Figure 11.11a)

Marquee Selection tools (Figure 11.11b)

Lasso tools (Figure 11.11c)

Quick Selection/Magic Wand tool (Figure 11.11d)

Crop tools (Figure 11.11e)

Eyedropper/Color Sampler/Measure/Count tools (Figure 11.11f)

Spot Healing Brush/Healing Brush/Patch/Red Eye tools (Figure 11.11g)

Brush/Pencil/Color Replacement/Mixer Brush tools (Figure 11.11h)

Clone Stamp/Pattern Stamp tools (Figure 11.11i)

History Brush/Art History Brush tool (Figure 11.11j)

Eraser/Background Eraser/Magic Eraser tools (Figure 11.11k)

Gradient/Paint Bucket tools (Figure 11.11l)

Blur/Sharpen/Smudge tools (Figure 11.11m)

Dodge/Burn/Sponge tools (Figure 11.11n)

Pen Path tools (Figure 11.11o)

Type/Type Mask tools (Figure 11.11p)

Path Selection/Direct Selection tools (Figure 11.11q)

Shape tools (Figure 11.11r)

3D Object tools (Figure 11.11s)

3D Camera tools (Figure 11.11t)

Hand/Rotate View tools (Figure 11.11u)

Zoom tool (Figure 11.11v)

Default Colors/Exchange Colors tools (Figure 11.11w)

Foreground Color/Background Color tools (Figure 11.11x)

Figure 1.12

Photoshop CS6 has a new interface, but the tool panels are very similar to Photoshop CS5. See Figures 1.13, which shows Photoshop CS5, and Figure 1.14, which shows Photoshop CS6, for a comparison of the interfaces. Generally speaking, changes in the new interface of a new version are cosmetic changes. The functions and the procedures of using these commands remain the same as in previous versions. If you know how to use Photoshop CS5, you will have no problem following CS6's new interface.

As with Photoshop CS5, if you pass the pointer over the buttons on the left side of your screen, you can see other command buttons. Figure 1.15 displays some of the command buttons in Photoshop CS6.

Summary

In this chapter, visual communication principles were introduced:

- Principle 1: Organize for visual perception.
- Principle 2: Guide the visual process.
- Principle 3: Clarify for visual complexity.
- Principle 4: Express visual meanings.

The chapter also briefly introduced Photoshop fundamentals.

Key Terms

Brightness
Color cues
Contrast
Grouping visual elements
Pop out
Primitive features
Texture segregation
Tools panel
Visual narrative

Reference

Malamed, Connie. Visual Language for Designers. Minneapolis: Rockport Publishers, Inc., 2009.

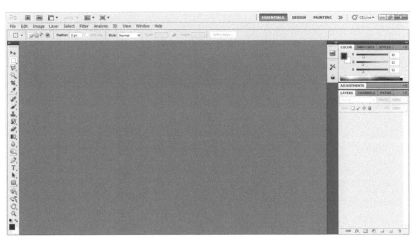

Figure 1.13

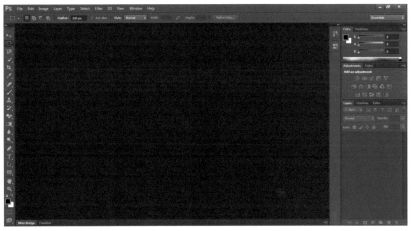

Figure 1.14

Figure 1.15

2

Working with Floor Plans and Elevations

Chapter 2 introduces techniques for creating floor plans and elevations using Photoshop. It describes the drawing creation process step-by-step. Both floor plans and elevations will be created with AutoCAD first. Then materials, lighting, background, and entourages will be added to both documents. The application of material and lighting (as well as adding entourages) is discussed thoroughly in the chapters that follow. The techniques and procedures are presented using simple demonstration examples. In this chapter, basic commands and tools are discussed to create a foundation for the material in the upcoming chapters.

AutoCAD is a software package used for drafting floor plans, elevations, and other two-dimensional drawings, as well as for 3D modeling. Photoshop is a powerful tool for enhancing images by adding colors, textures, materials, and lighting effects, as well as other special effects. To use the drawings created in AutoCAD, you need to export your drawings to EPS (Encapsulated PostScript) format so they can be read in Photoshop. You also can plot your file from AutoCAD to PDF (Portable Document File) format. However, EPS is recommended because, unlike PDF, it retains different line weights. In addition, you will be asked to specify the resolution when you open the EPS file in Photoshop. Opening a PDF file requires rasterizing, which changes the file content, resulting in a lower resolution. EPS and TIF (Tagged Image File) formats are much more common, as they preserve file quality. Note that if your EPS file is not visible when you try to open it in Photoshop, you can use the Rectangular Marquee tool to select the drawing and copy it to a new file in Photoshop.

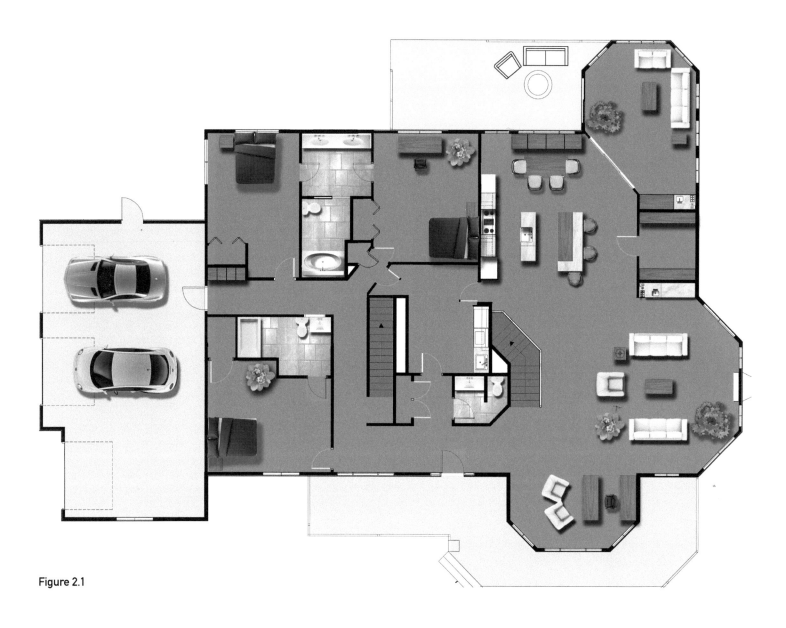

Figure 2.1

Working with Floor Plans

The floor plan is a visual component in a presentation drawing or presentation board that you include to show spatial relationships. Floor plans in presentation drawings are different from floor plans in construction documents. In a presentation board or drawing, the floor plan is used for communicating the spatial relationship, the design concept, the color scheme, and the design style. Therefore, materials and colors must be included, but, unlike construction documents, technical information such as dimensions and coded notes are not necessary. Figure 2.1 is a house floor plan that presents different materials and colors. Entourages, such as cars and plants, are included to provide a sense of scale.

In Figure 2.1, the visual communication principles discussed in Chapter 1 are applied. In order to make the furniture pop out from the background, a gray color was used for the entire floor. The furniture is presented in photos, not drawings or models, and show actual materials and texture. The floor materials also are shown with

photographed materials and texture. As discussed in the previous chapter, the segregation of the texture makes objects pop out. The following describes the procedure of creating the floor plan with Photoshop.

Overview of the Floor Plan Creation Process

The next section goes in-depth into the process, giving the detailed step-by-step procedure. For now, the following is a description of the overall process of creating and enhancing a floor plan:

1. In AutoCAD, export the file to an EPS file format. Then open it in Photoshop
2. Choose the color for a background that will cover the entire floor.
3. Apply real materials to the furniture.
4. Find photos for each object.
5. Add entourages, such as plants and cars.
6. Add shadows to each object.

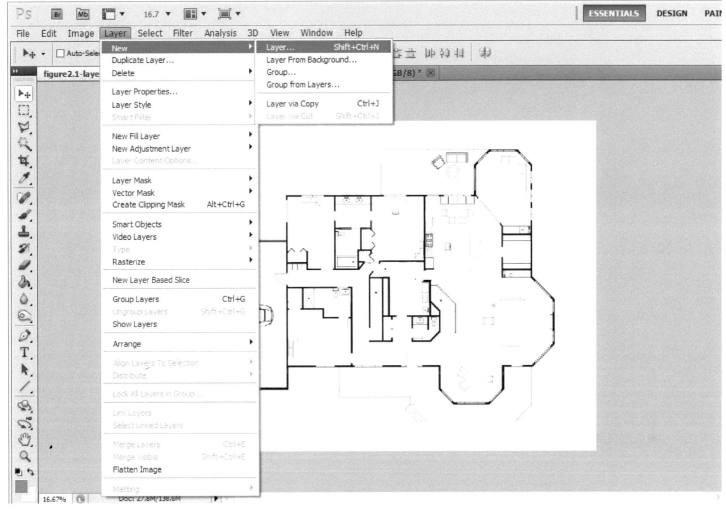

Figure 2.2

Creating a Floor Plan Using Photoshop

Before proceeding with a demonstration of the drawing creation process, you must understand the layers concept.

Layers

Layers play an essential role in all aspects of Photoshop work. Working with layers lets you keep various elements in a design separate from each other. You also can turn individual layers on and off to make a particular image visible or invisible. Layers also allow you to construct an image in stages and maintain the flexibility to make any editing changes you want at a later stage.

Putting each object on a separate layer is crucial in your drawing creation process. For example, you might need to add shadows to each of the objects. Only separate layers make doing this easy.

To rename a layer in Photoshop, simply double-click the layer name. Then type the new name in the box.

1. Open the AutoCAD drawing that is in PDF format in Photoshop. Create a new layer for the background. Go to Layer > New > Layer. See Figure 2.2.

The dialogue box shown in Figure 2.3 appears. Create a new layer called "Background-fill."

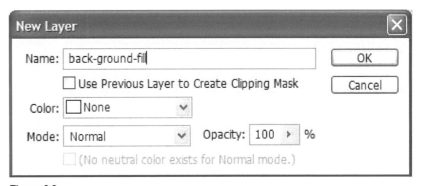

Figure 2.3

Click OK. A new layer appears in the Layers panel on the right side of the screen (see Figure 2.4). In order to edit an object on a layer, you must make the layer active. Select the layer. Note in Figure 2.4, "Background-fill" has been highlighted to make it the active layer. Rename "Layer 1" as "line-drawing."

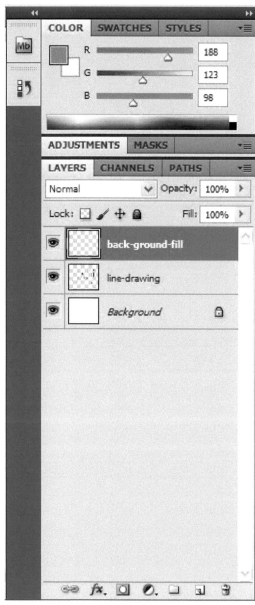

Figure 2.4

Magic Wand Tool

2. Use the **Magic Wand tool** to select the area you will fill in with gray. (The Magic Wand tool is the fourth button from the top in the Tools panel located at the left of your screen.) When you click on the area with the Magic Wand, the area is highlighted with dashed lines, as shown in Figure 2.5. If you need to select more than one area, hold the Shift key and click on more than one area. When you select the area, you need to make the "line-drawing" layer active.

Paint Bucket Tool

3. Use the **Paint Bucket tool** to fill gray color for the background. This feature can be accessed from the Tools panel. Before applying color to the desired area, specify the color you want by clicking on "Foreground Color/Background Color" as shown in Figure 1.11x. You are then prompted by the dialogue box shown in Figure 2.6.

4. Click OK. Use the Paint Bucket tool to apply gray to the selected areas. You can also use a different color to fill in the staircase. Remember to make the "background-fill" layer active so that your colors appear on the layer. Your floor plan should look like Figure 2.7.

Rectangular Marquee Tool

5. Next, fill in the material for all the tables. You can download an image of wood from the Internet and use Edit > Transform > Scale to change the scale of the wood. Use the **Rectangular Marquee tool** (the second tool button on the Tools panel) to select the wood. Then go to Edit > Transform > Scale, as shown in Figure 2.8.

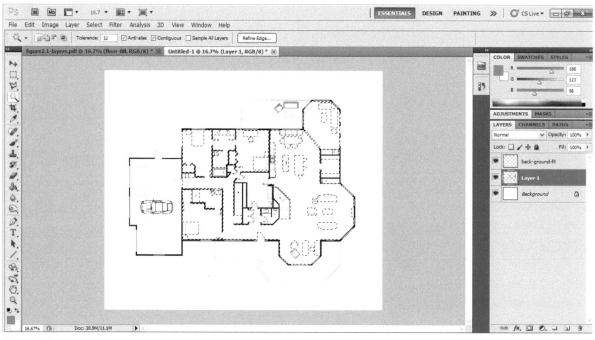

Figure 2.5

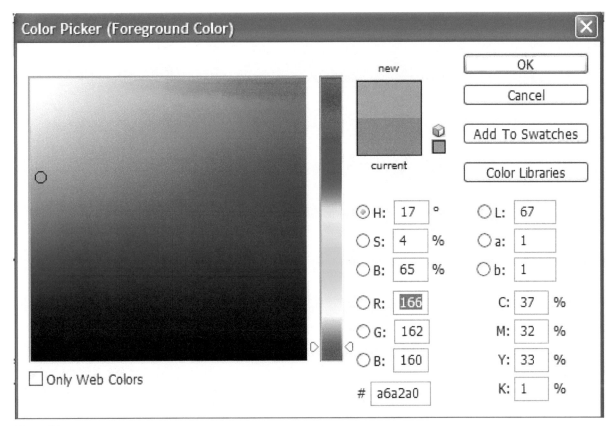

Figure 2.6

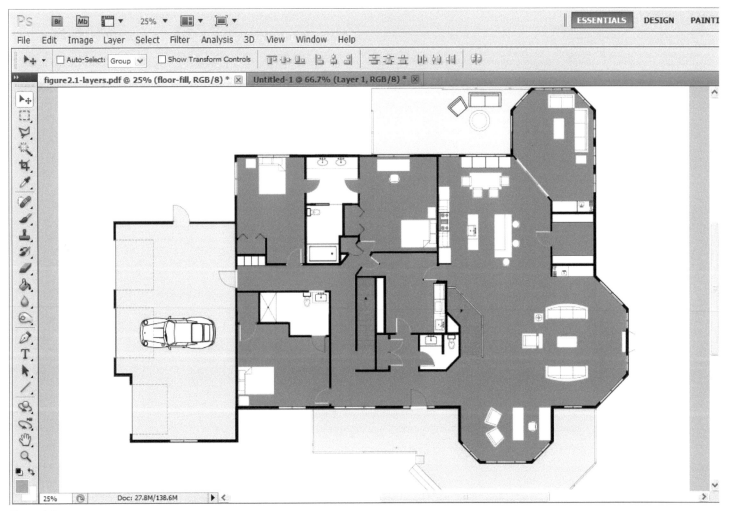

Figure 2.7

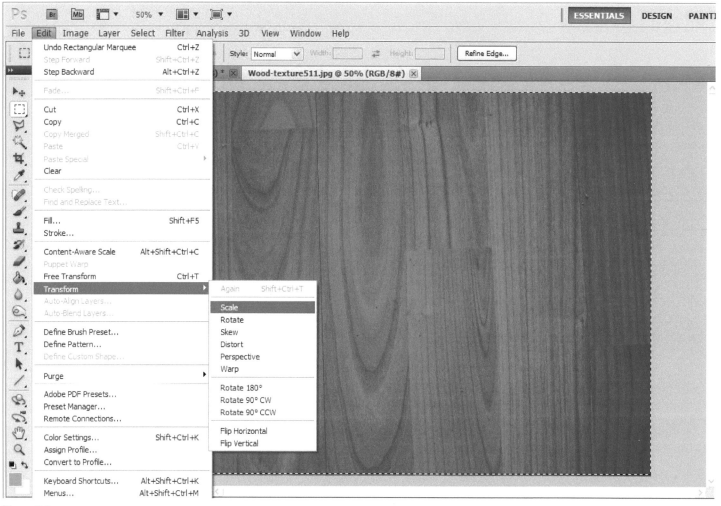

Figure 2.8

Transform > Scale

Eight small squares should now appear around the edge of the wood image. You can click on one of the corner squares to scale it up or down. In Figure 2.9, the wood image has been scaled down to a smaller size. After you press Enter, the command is completed; you can then use Ctrl + D to deselect the wood image. It is crucial to understand the scale and proportion of the material that you are applying to your drawing. For example, the wood grain scale needs to match how it would fit in the table or fit in a space that size. **Transform > Scale** allows you to adjust the scale of the material that you apply.

6. In your wood image file, use the Rectangular Marquee tool to select the scaled-down wood image. Then go to Edit > Copy.
7. Open your floor plan and use the Magic Wand tool to select one table. Then go to Edit > Paste Special > Paste Into, as shown in Figure 2.10.
8. After you paste the wood image into the table, a new layer is added to the Layers panel. Rename the layer "wood-1," as shown in Figure 2.11.
9. Repeat the same procedure to apply wood material on all wood tables. You also can apply bathroom floor tile to the floor plan using the same procedure. The floor plan should now look like Figure 2.12.

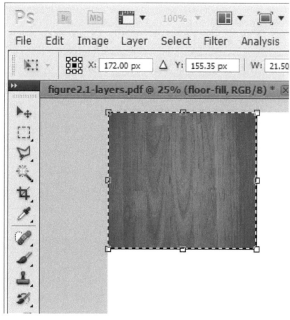

Figure 2.9

10. Not only can you scale materials, but also you can scale photos. For example, the bed, plants, cars, and sofas in these figures are all photos that have been scaled and placed in the floor plan. The procedure is the same as described above.

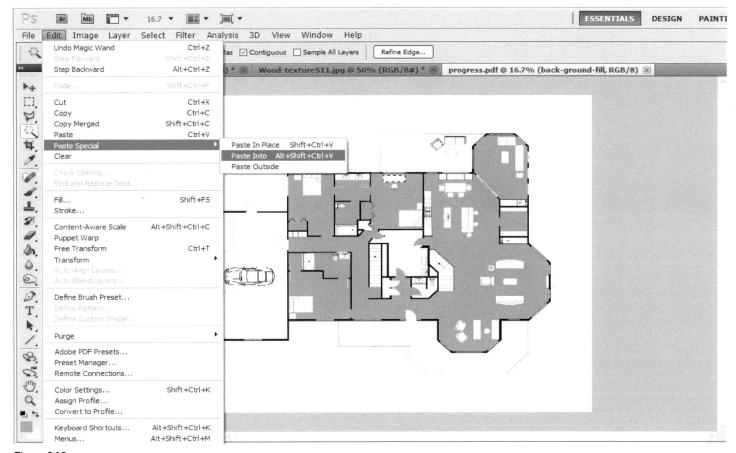

Figure 2.10

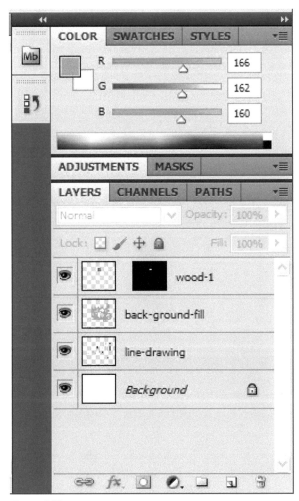

Figure 2.11

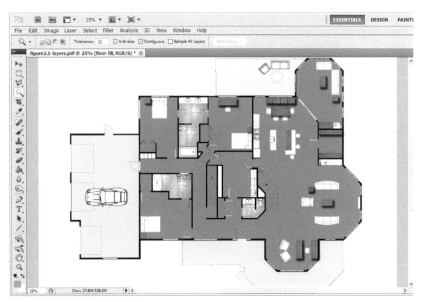

Figure 2.12

Select Inverse

11. Now bring a photo to your floor plan. Open the "bed" photo in Photoshop. Then click on the background (white area) with the Magic Wand tool. You can hold the Shift key to select more than one area. After you select all areas you want, right-click on the bed photo; a pull-down menu appears. Highlight Select Inverse, as shown in Figure 2.13. The bed and pillows are now selected, as shown in Figure 2.14.

Figure 2.13

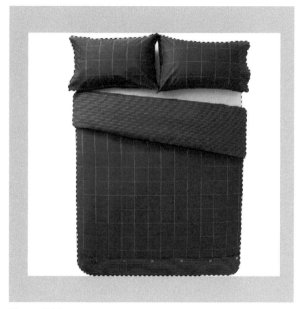

Figure 2.14

12. Select Edit > Copy. Then open your floor plan, click on it, and select Edit > Paste. You can use the same procedure as described above to scale the bed to fit on the floor plan.

13. After you paste the bed in the floor plan, rename the layer "double-bed-1." When all three beds are

pasted in the floor plan, you can use the Move tool to move the bed to the desired location. When you use this tool, make sure the layer with the object is active. At this point, the drawing looks like Figure 2.15. Note the layers also shown in the figure.

Drop Shadows

14. Notice that there are shadows under the beds and tables in the floor plan. To add the shadows, go to Layer > Layer Style > **Drop Shadow**, as shown in Figure 2.16, making sure the layer with the object is currently active. Note that it is important to

Figure 2.15

bookshelf in the drawing, as shown in Figure 2.39. Select Edit > Transform > Scale to change the size of the photo for each object and fit it into your drawing.

12. Create a separate layer called "sofa." Select Copy > Paste to add a sofa, as shown in Figure 2.40. Select Edit > Transform > Scale to change the size of the photo and fit it into your drawing.

13. Add entourages, such as human figures. Create separate layers called "human-figure-1" and

"human-figure-2." Select Copy > Paste to add human figures, as shown in Figure 2.41. Select Edit > Transform > Scale to change the size of the figure to fit into your drawing.

14. Add shadows to each object to create a sense of depth. To add the shadow, use the Layer > Layer Style > Drop Shadow option as discussed in the floor plan instructions at the beginning of the chapter. You also can adjust the values for each setting in order to create different shadow effects.

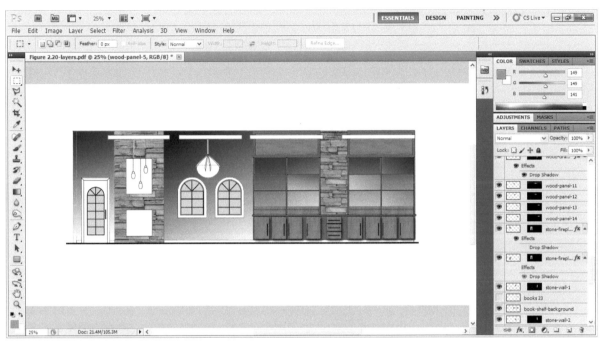

Figure 2.36

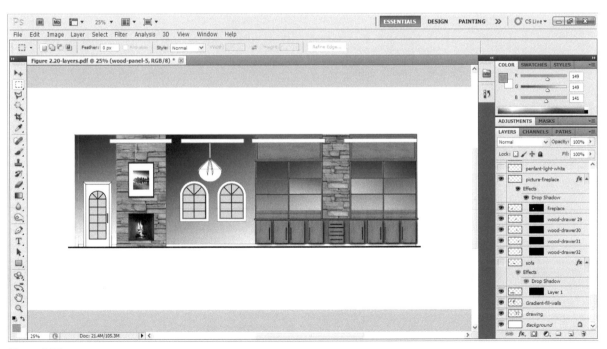

Figure 2.37

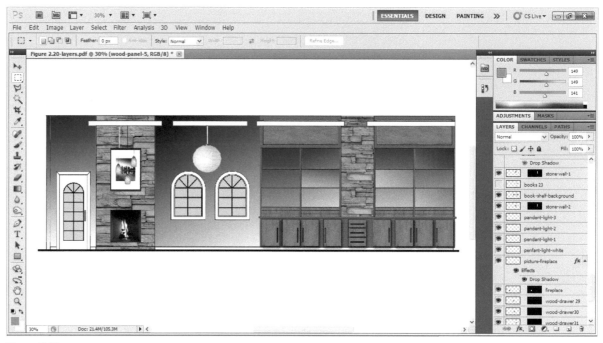

Figure 2.38

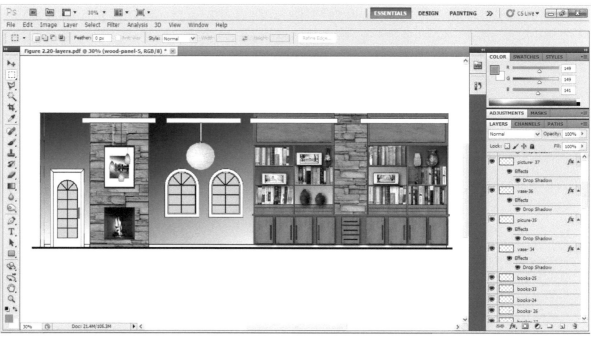

Figure 2.39

Summary

In this chapter, both the floor plan and interior elevations were created with Photoshop. In addition to basic techniques and tools, such as the Paint Bucket and Gradient Fill, adding materials and textures to drawings was demonstrated. Topics included the following:

- Bringing photos to a drawing

- Using Transform > Scale to scale the photos

- Bringing photographed materials to a drawing using the Copy > Paste Into command

- Bringing entourages, such as human figures, plants, and cars, into a drawing

Key Terms

Copy > Paste
Copy > Paste Into
Drop Shadows
Entourage
Gradient Fill tool
Layers
Layer Style
Magic Wand tool
Move tool
Paint Bucket tool
Rectangular Marquee tool
Select Inverse
Transform > Scale

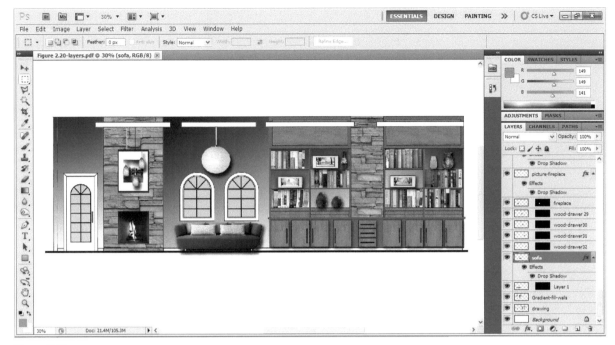

Figure 2.40

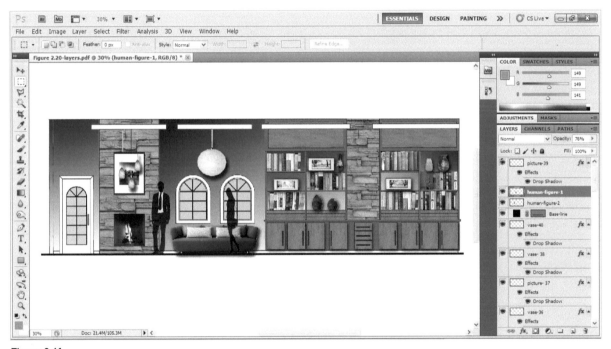

Figure 2.41

Projects

1. Use the floor plan provided on the book's
    companion website http://www.bloomsbury.com/us/
    photoshop-for-interior-designers-9781609015442/
    to add colors, materials, and textures to the floor
    plan in Photoshop. Add entourages to your floor
    plan as well.
2. Use the elevation provided on the book's
    companion website to add materials as well
    as colors to the elevation in Photoshop. Add
    entourages to your elevation as well.

3

Working with Perspectives and Isometric Views

Chapter 3 introduces techniques of creating perspective and isometric drawings using Photoshop. It describes the drawing creation process step-by-step. Perspective and isometric drawings present three-dimensional views of a space, which help viewers to understand spatial relationships. These drawings sometimes include the color scheme and material selection, as well as the style of the design. The multi-software method is introduced in this chapter, allowing the designer to produce perspective and isometric drawings quickly. As mentioned, the multi-software approach refers to using 3D AutoCAD, 3D Studio Max, Trimble SketchUp, Revit, or other 3D software to generate preliminary 3D models first and then refining these models in Photoshop by adding materials, shadows, lighting, and furniture and accessories.

Readers are expected to have some knowledge of perspective, including such concepts as one-point perspective, two-point perspective, and the vanishing point. Understanding basic perspective concepts ensures you can import furniture and artwork into the correct scale of the preliminary models.

Working with Perspective Views

Figure 3.1 is a perspective view of a retail space that has been enhanced by Photoshop. The view was initially created in Trimble SketchUp, shown in Figure 3.2. With this software, partial materials and furniture were placed in the drawing. In Figure 3.2, the lines on the floor represent the furniture layout, which was imported from an AutoCAD file. When working in Trimble SketchUp, you need not draw a floor plan from scratch; instead, you can import it from your AutoCAD drawing. Note that if you are using an older version of SketchUp, you need to save your AutoCAD floor plan to TIF or JPG format to import it. Newer versions allow you to import an AutoCAD file from DWG format. Be sure to clean up your floor plan and purge unused layers, blocks, and references in AutoCAD before you import it.

Creating a Perspective View in SketchUp

To create a perspective view of this retail space:

1. Import the floor plan from AutoCAD file to Trimble SketchUp. The importing process is described in detail in Chapter 10.
2. In Trimble SketchUp, build vertical walls, bring in furniture from 3D Warehouse, and apply materials on the wall from the Material library. This process is also covered in detail in Chapter 10.

Figure 3.1

Figure 3.2

3. Create a perspective view of the retail space in Trimble SketchUp using the Position Camera feature.
4. Save the perspective view in Trimble SketchUp in a TIF or JPG file using the Export-2D Graphics feature, as shown in Figure 3.2.
5. Open Figure 3.2 in Photoshop. Use the Clone Stamp tool to clean up the floor (i.e., to erase all lines brought in from AutoCAD; although you cleaned up the file in AutoCAD, some additional removal of residue will be necessary).
6. Create different layers for different objects, such as "track-lighting-1," "track-lighting-2," and "picture-1," and so on.
7. Obtain and prepare images of track lighting, lighting fixtures, framed pictures, and any other furniture and accessories you want to include.
8. Bring each of these objects to your Photoshop drawing by using Edit > Copy and Edit > Paste. Then scale to the proper perspective by using Edit > Transform > Scale or Edit > Transform > Perspective.
9. Add lighting effects on the wall by using **Filter > Render > Lighting Effects**.
10. Create shadows by using the Drop Shadow layer style, the Lasso tool, and the Paint Bucket tool, or by using the Gradient Fill tool.
11. Bring human figures into your drawing to present a sense of scale by using Edit > Copy and Edit > Paste. Then scale the figures to the proper size by using Edit > Transform > Scale or Edit > Transform > Perspective.

Creating a Perspective View Using Photoshop

As described in the previous chapter, creating different layers for different objects is essential, as it allows you to change, delete, or modify objects individually, adding, for example, a drop shadow to each. The following explores how to bring a framed picture to your perspective drawing in Photoshop and how to add lighting effects on the wall. (Note: A more detailed discussion of lighting is in Chapter 5.)

Using the Clone Stamp Tool

Because the perspective view was created in Trimble SketchUp and the floor plan was brought in from an AutoCAD file, some lines will need to be erased before you refine your perspective in Photoshop (see Figure 3.2). You cannot use the Eraser tool to erase the lines because it will erase the gray pixels, leaving white. Instead, you'll need to use the **Clone Stamp tool** to copy the gray color of the floor plan over the lines. The Clone Stamp tool is located on the left side, in the Tools panel, as shown in Figure 3.3.

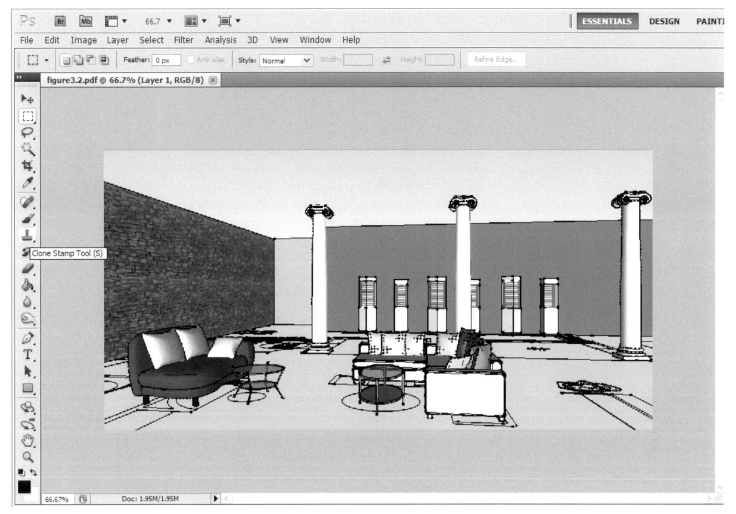

Figure 3.3

The Clone Stamp tool paints one part of an image over another part of the same image or over another part of any open document that has the same color mode. You can also paint part of one layer over another layer. This tool is useful for duplicating objects or removing a defect in an image. To use the Clone Stamp tool, set a sampling point on the area you want to copy (clone) the pixels from and paint over another area.

You can use any brush tip with this tool as long as it gives you precise control over the size of the clone area. To change the brush tip and size, use the drop-down menu as shown in Figure 3.4. You can also use Opacity and Flow settings to control how paint is applied to the cloned area. These settings are at the top of your screen as shown in Figure 3.4.

Following are steps for the Clone Stamp tool:

1. Select the Clone Stamp tool.
2. Choose a brush tip and set brush options for the blending mode, opacity, and flow in the Options bar.
3. Hold down the Alt key and use the Clone Stamp tool to copy the sample you want to use. In this case, copy the gray color on the floor.

4. Move the Clone Stamp tool to the area you want to correct. In this case, use the Clone Stamp tool to erase the lines on the floor.

The corrected drawing should look like Figure 3.5.

Adding a Framed Picture to a Perspective Drawing

Instead of creating a 3D model for a framed picture for your model, you can bring a framed picture to your perspective drawing in Photoshop. This is a quick way to refine your perspective drawing. The procedure is as follows:

1. Obtain and prepare a framed picture you want to use.
2. Open the picture in Photoshop, using the Rectangular Marquee tool to select the framed picture and the Copy command, as shown in Figure 3.6.
3. Open your perspective drawing in Photoshop, and then paste the framed picture in the perspective drawing, as shown in Figure 3.7. Rename the layer "picture-1."

Figure 3.4

Figure 3.5

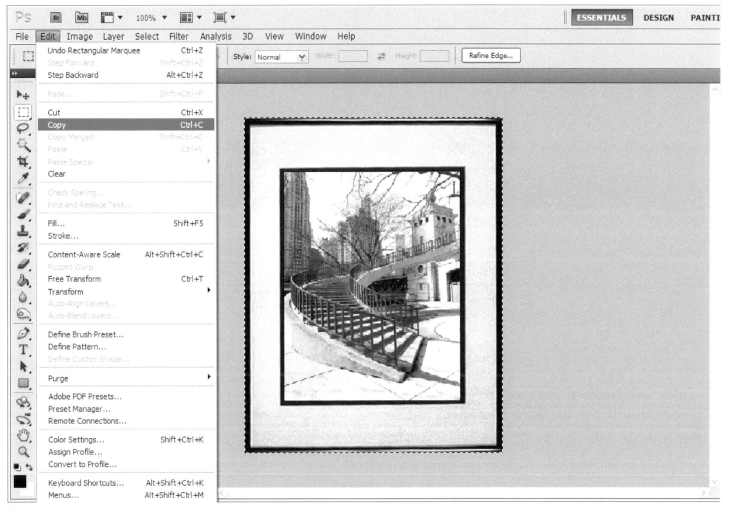

Figure 3.6

Figure 3.7

4. Use the Rectangular Marquee tool to select the framed picture, then use Edit > Transform > Scale to adjust the size and proportion of the framed picture. In this case, scale down the size and adjust the proportion of the framed picture (see Figure 3.8).

5. Use **Edit > Transform > Perspective** to create the framed picture in a perspective view, as shown in Figure 3.9. Use **Edit > Transform > Distort** to adjust the perspective and proportion of the framed picture, as shown in Figure 3.10.

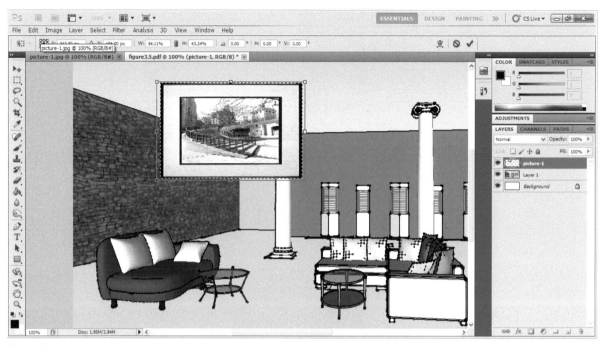

Figure 3.8

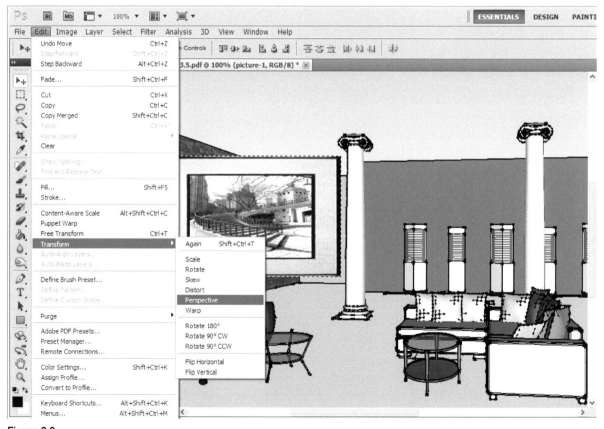

Figure 3.9

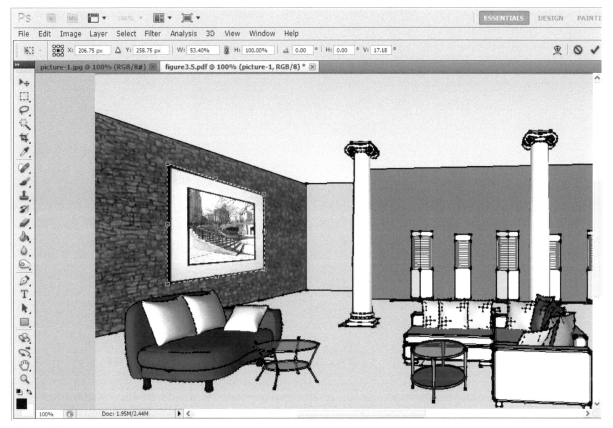

Figure 3.10

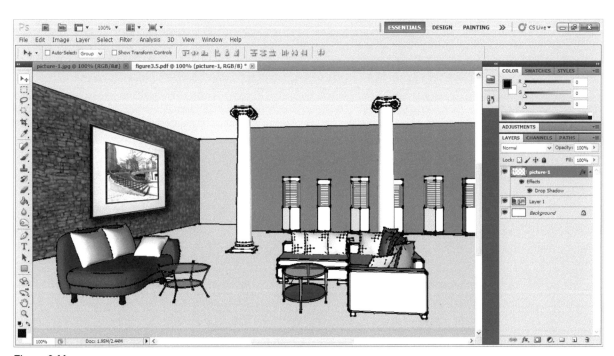

Figure 3.11

6. Use Layer > Layer Style > Drop Shadow to add shadow to the framed picture. The drawing should look like Figure 3.11.

Adding Track Lighting to a Perspective Drawing

Adding track lighting to a perspective drawing is similar to that used in Chapter 2 to add books and other accessories to the interior elevation. However, in this case you need to pay attention to the perspective effect in perspective drawing. You can use Edit > Transform > Perspective or Edit > Transform > Distort to adjust the size, proportion, and location of the object. When selecting track lighting in Photoshop, make sure you right-click and choose Select Inverse to select the object only (Figure 3.12). Otherwise, you will copy the white background to your perspective drawing.

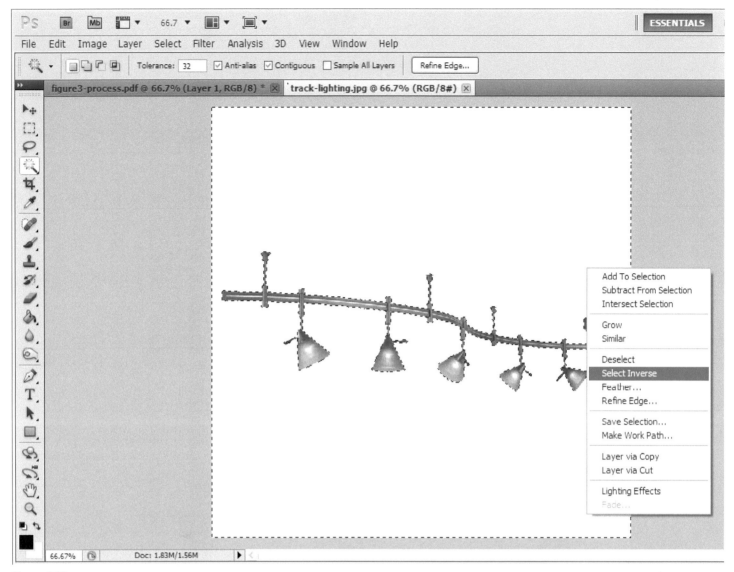

Figure 3.12

Figure 3.13

After you paste two track lighting fixtures in your perspective drawing, your drawing should look like Figure 3.13. Make sure to rename the layers "track-lighting-1" and "track-lighting-2" to help organize them.

Adding Lighting Effects to the Wall

You also can add lighting effects to your Photoshop drawings to make them look more realistic. More detailed information about this as well as the corresponding procedure are introduced in Chapter 5. For now, however, follow these steps:

1. In your perspective drawing, make layer-1 active; go to Filter > Render > Lighting Effects as shown in Figure 3.14.
2. Highlight Lighting Effects. A dialogue box appears, as shown in Figure 3.15.

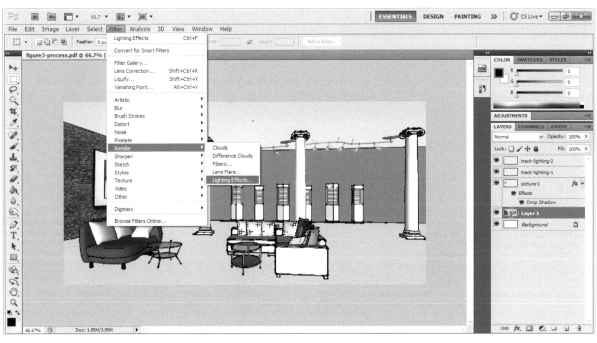

Figure 3.14

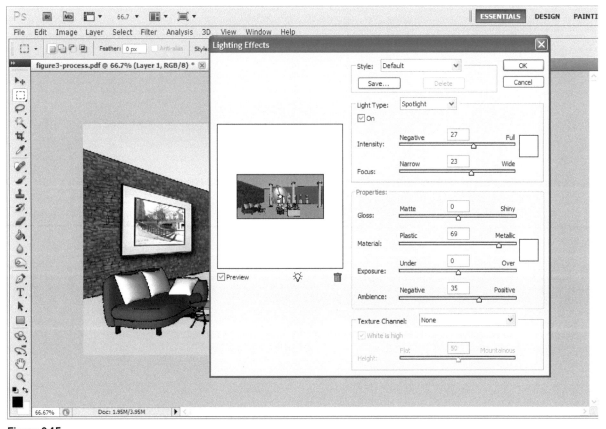

Figure 3.15

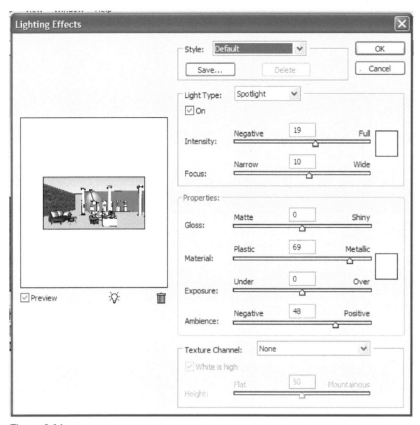

Figure 3.16

3. Choose Light Type as **Spotlight**; adjust the Intensity, Focus, and Ambience values (described in the list that follows) in the dialogue box as shown in Figure 3.16. The white circle at the center of the ellipse (see Figure 3.17) defines the center point of the light and is used to reposition the light within the preview window. All four points within the ellipse can be used to change the size and shape of the ellipse. Following are the values of the spotlight:

- **Intensity:** Regulates how much light is emitted from the source. Drag the slider to the right to increase light or to the left to decrease it.

- **Focus:** Defines how much of the ellipse is filled with light. Drag the slider to the right to fill the ellipse or to the left to restrict the spread of light.

- **Ambience:** Factors in the scene's other light sources, such as daylight or artificial lights, and diffuses the created light with those light sources. Drag toward Positive to increase this type of light or toward Negative to decrease it.

4. Click OK. Your drawing should look like Figure 3.17.
5. Repeat the same procedure for the rest of the lighting effects on the back wall. After you add three more spotlights, your drawing will look like Figure 3.18.

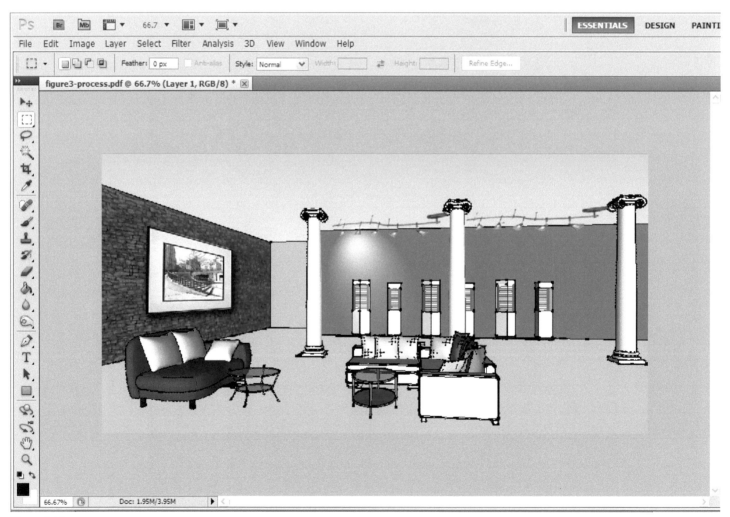

Figure 3.17

Figure 3.18

Creating Shadows on the Floor

Adding shadows is important to create a sense of both distance and depth of space in your drawing. If the furniture and objects are added in Photoshop, it is easy to add shadows by using the **Drop Shadow layer style** or other features in the software. However, sometimes you must create shadows manually. More detailed information on this topic appears in Chapter 5. In the meantime, the focus is the perspective drawing currently under construction in this chapter. The furniture was added in Trimble SketchUp. Use the **Lasso tool** to draw the outline of the

shadow, making sure that the shadow outlines match the perspective effect in your perspective drawing. That means the vanishing points of your shadow outlines should be the same as the vanishing points for the space and objects. The procedure for creating this effect is as follows:

1. Create a layer called "Shadow" in your perspective drawing.
2. Click on Lasso tool, as shown in Figure 3.19.
3. Use the Lasso tool to draw shadow outlines on the floor, as shown in Figure 3.20. Hold the Shift key down when drawing multiple outlines.

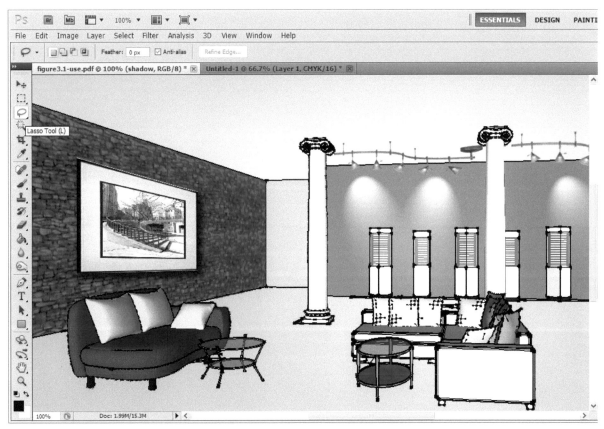

Figure 3.19

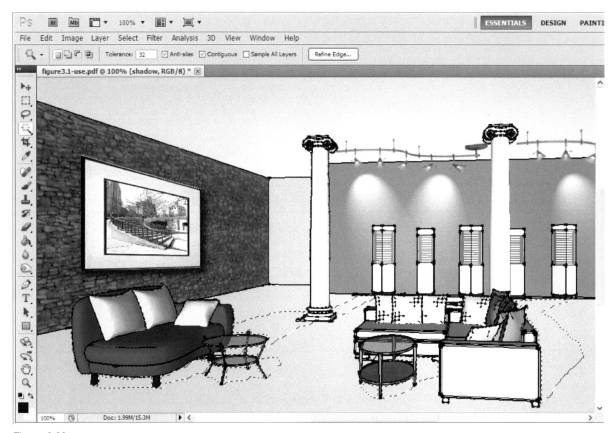

Figure 3.20

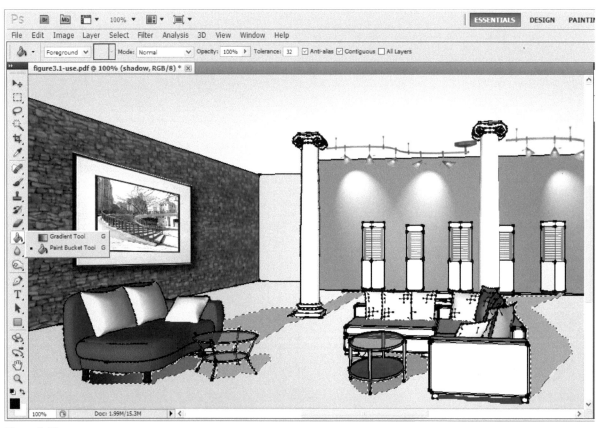

Figure 3.21

Figure 3.22

4. Use the Paint Bucket or Gradient Fill tool to fill in gray color within the shadow outlines, as shown in Figure 3.21.

Adding Other Objects to a Perspective Drawing

Adding other objects to your perspective drawing requires you to create separate layers for each object, as shown in Figure 3.22. You can add the second framed picture, the chandelier, vases, as well as the display case. After you add all the objects, your drawing should look like Figure 3.22.

Adding Human Figures to a Perspective Drawing

Adding entourages to a perspective drawing not only adds interest to your drawing but also provides a sense of scale and distance. By adding human figures of different sizes at various places, you will enhance the discernment of distance in an interior space. To do so, follow these steps:

1. Create a layer called "people."
2. Open a human figure drawing in Photoshop. Use the Magic Wand tool to click on the background. Then right-click and highlight Select Inverse, as shown in Figure 3.23. Note that only two people will be selected, not the white background, as shown in Figure 3.24.

Figure 3.23

3. Open your perspective drawing and make the "people" layer active. Use Edit > Paste to add the human figures to the perspective drawing. Use Edit > Transform > Scale to adjust the size of the figures. Change the Opacity value by adjusting the slider to make your human figures in a gray tone, as shown in Figure 3.25. The Opacity option is located at the

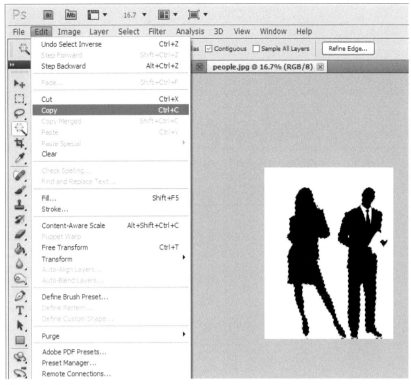

Figure 3.24

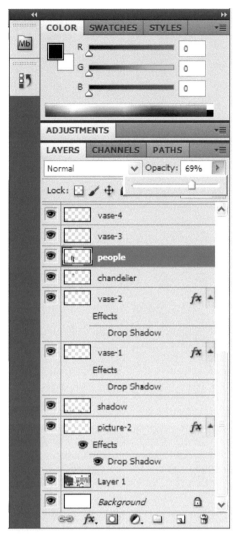

top of the Layers panel on the right side of your screen, as shown in Figure 3.26.

4. Create another layer called "people-talking." Use the same procedure as Step 3 to add these two figures to your drawing. These people are farther away from the viewer and should therefore be smaller than the first two to provide a sense of distance. See Figure 3.27.

Figure 3.26

Figure 3.25

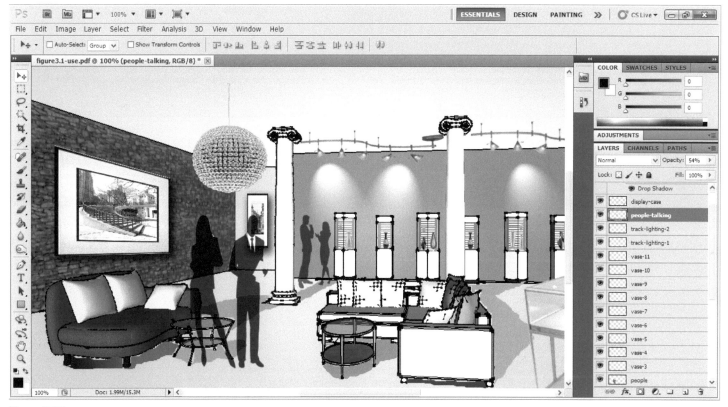

Figure 3.27

Creating an Exterior View in a Perspective Drawing

Adding an exterior view to your perspective drawing is another way to enhance it. Doing so not only creates a sense of distance, it also presents a sense of the environmental setting of the interior space. Figure 3.28 is an example of interior perspective with an exterior view added. The steps to add an exterior view follow.

Figure 3.28

1. The interior perspective was created in Trimble SketchUp. No furniture has been added to the drawing as shown in Figure 3.29. Save the file as a PDF document.

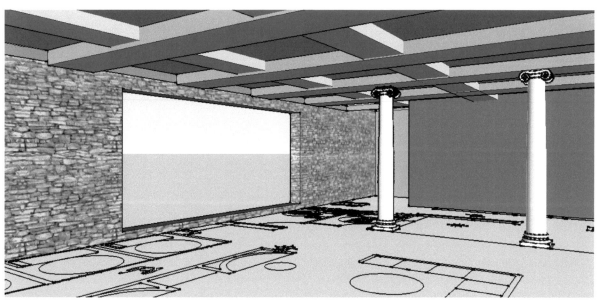

Figure 3.29

2. Open Figure 3.29 in Photoshop. Use the Clone Stamp tool to clean up lines on the floor. Your drawing should look like Figure 3.30.

3. Open the exterior view photo in Photoshop. Use the Rectangular Marquee tool to select the photo. Then use Edit > Copy to copy the photo as shown in Figure 3.31.

4. Open your perspective drawing. Use Edit > Paste to add the exterior view photo. Use the Rectangular Marquee tool to select the photo. Go to Edit > Transform > Scale to scale the photo to a desired size, as shown in Figure 3.32.

5. Use Edit > Transform > Distort to adjust the photo to match the vanishing point in your perspective drawing, as shown in Figure 3.33.

6. Use Distort to adjust the exterior view photo to match the window on the wall, as shown in Figure 3.34.

7. Rename the layer "Exterior-view." Draw window mullions by using the Square shape tool and the Paint Bucket tool. At this point, your perspective should look like Figure 3.35.

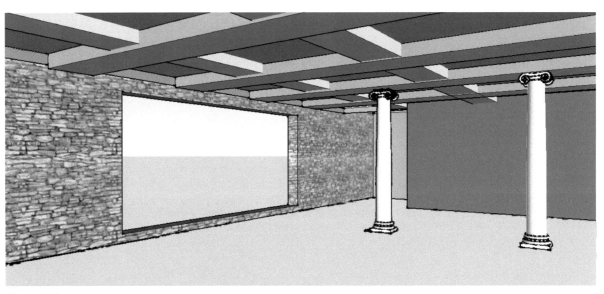

Figure 3.30

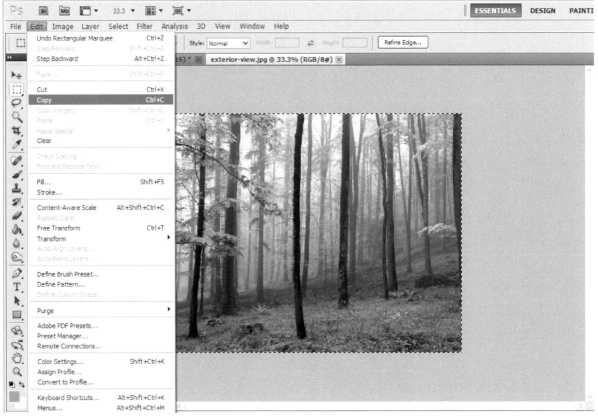

Figure 3.31

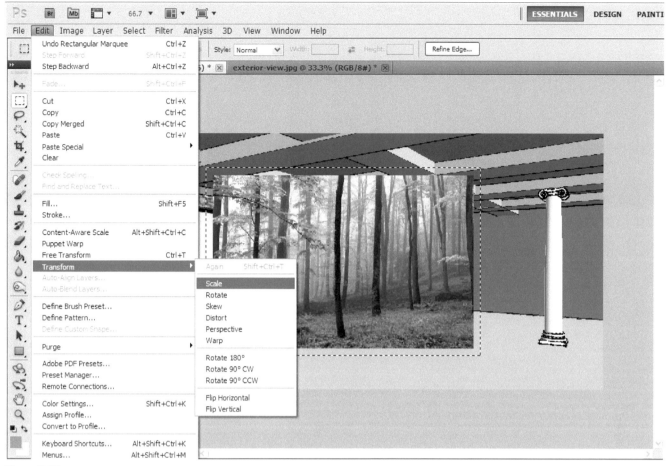

Figure 3.32

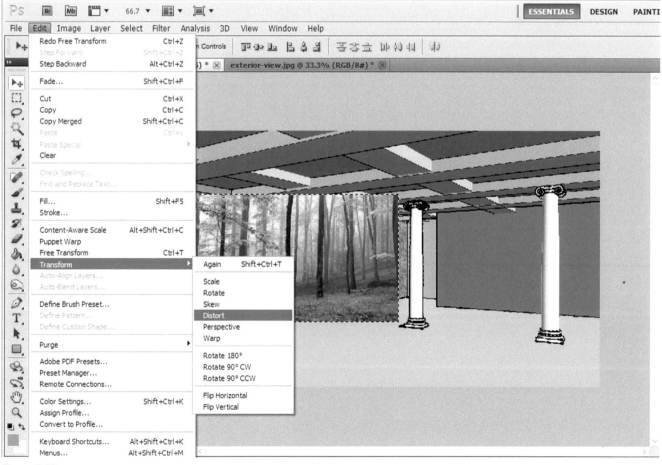

Figure 3.33

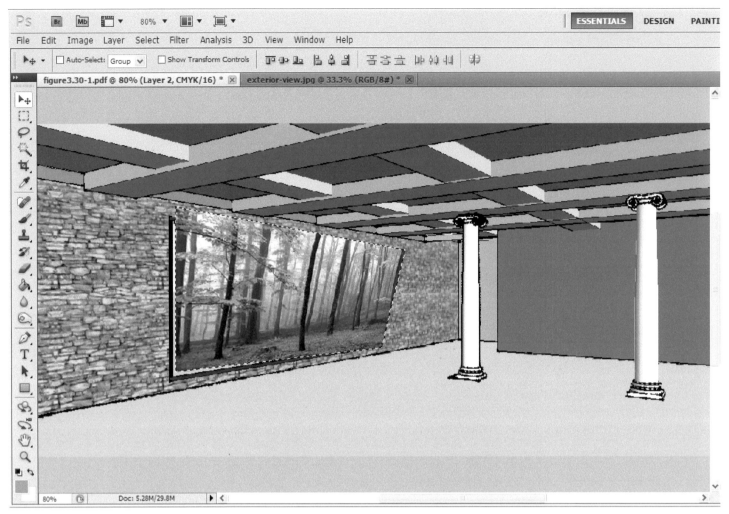

Figure 3.34

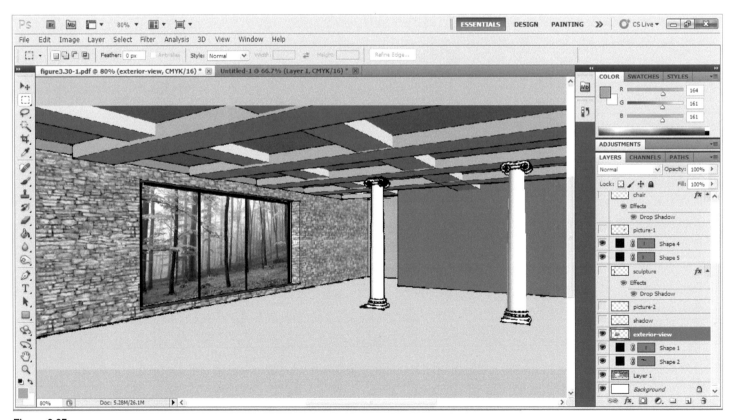

Figure 3.35

Applying Materials on the Wall in Perspective

Figure 4.22 is another perspective view of the retail space that has been enhanced by Photoshop. The perspective view was originally created in Trimble SketchUp, as shown in Figure 4.23. The wood wall material, furniture, wallpaper, and human figures as well as the exterior view were added using Photoshop.

The procedure of applying material on the wall is as follows:

1. Obtain and prepare the wall material you are going to use.
2. Open the TIF format perspective drawing in Photoshop, as shown in Figure 4.23.
3. Use the Gradient Fill tool to fill in gray color in the ceiling area, as shown in Figure 4.24.
4. Open the wall material in Photoshop. Use the Rectangular Marquee tool to select the wall material. Then use Edit > Copy to copy the wall material, as shown in Figure 4.25.
5. Open the perspective drawing in Photoshop. Use the Magic Wand tool to select the area to which you are going to apply wall material. Then use Edit > Paste Special > Paste Into to paste the wall material, as shown in Figure 4.26.
6. After pasting the wall material on the wall, use the Rectangular Marquee tool to select the wall material. Then use **Edit > Transform > Perspective** to adjust the perspective of the material to match the perspective of your drawing. You can drag the small squares to adjust your perspective, as shown in Figure 4.27.
7. You also can use Edit > Transform > Scale to make the material bigger to fit into the wall. If you need to move the material, use the Move tool to move the material to the desired location, as shown in Figure 4.28. It is important to adjust both perspective and scale for the pattern of the material you are bringing into the 3D model.
8. Use the Magic Wand tool to select the area again. Then use Edit > Paste Special > Paste Into to paste the wall material into the rest of the area. You can use the same method to adjust the size and perspective for the material, as shown in Figure 4.29.
9. Open the birch tree wallpaper image in Photoshop. Use the Rectangular Marquee tool to select birch tree wallpaper, and then use Edit > Copy to copy the image, as shown in Figure 4.30.
10. Open the perspective drawing in Photoshop. Use the Magic Wand tool to select the area in which you are going to paste birch tree wallpaper. Hold down the Shift key to select multiple areas. Then use Edit > Paste Special > Paste Into to paste in

Figure 4.22

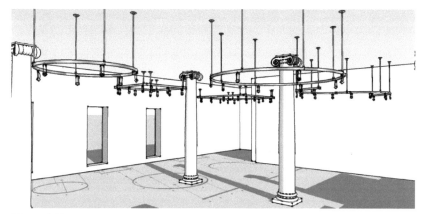

Figure 4.23

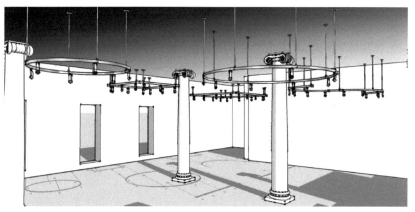

Figure 4.24

the wallpaper. Your drawing should look like Figure 4.31. Since the birch tree wallpaper has a repeat pattern, it is important to make sure that the patterns repeat in correct perspective and scale.

11. Use the Rectangular Marquee tool to select the entire birch tree wallpaper. Then use Edit > Transform > Perspective to adjust the perspective of the wall material. You can drag the small squares to match the perspective in the drawing, as shown in Figure 4.32.
12. Bring a sofa into your perspective. Make sure to create a new layer for the sofa. The method is the same as described in the previous chapter. See Figure 4.33.

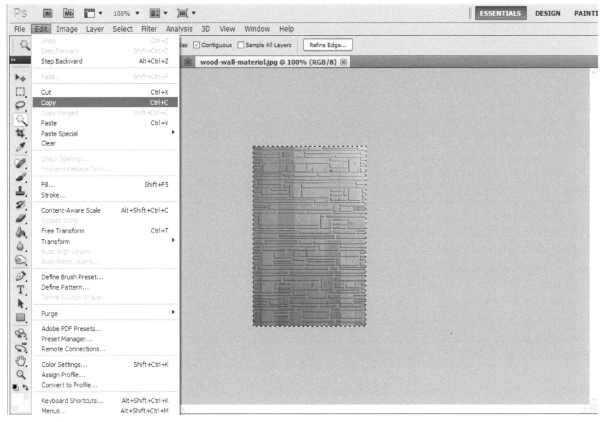

Figure 4.25

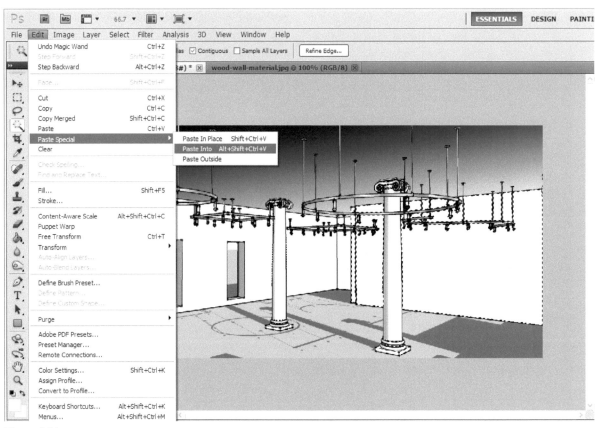

Figure 4.26

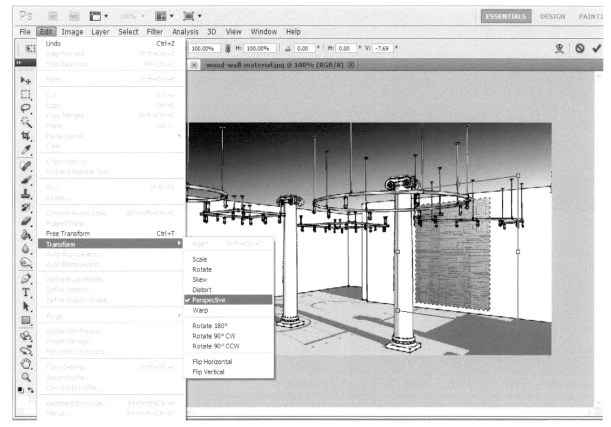

Figure 4.27

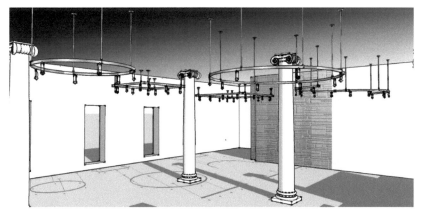

Figure 4.28

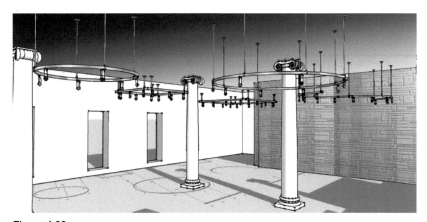

Figure 4.29

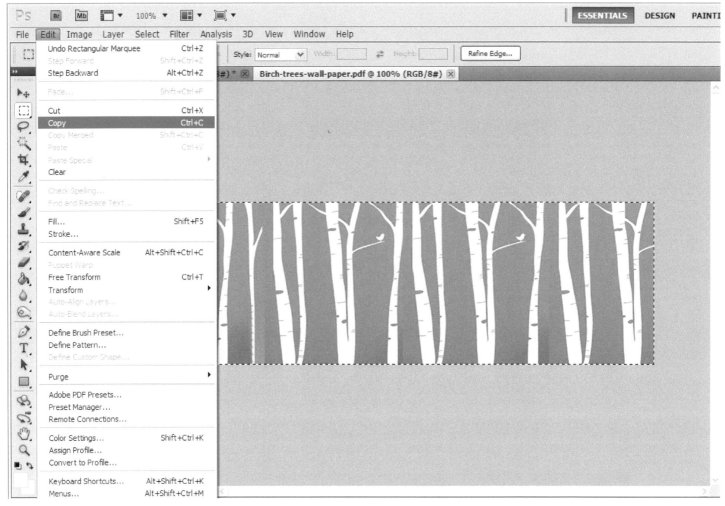

Figure 4.30

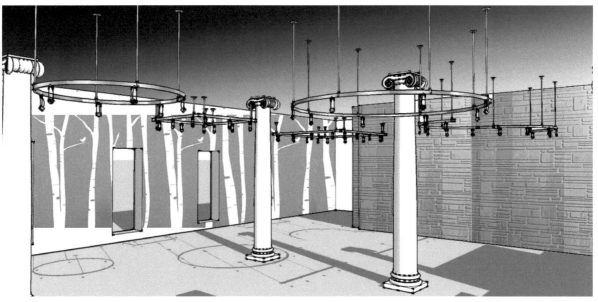

Figure 4.31

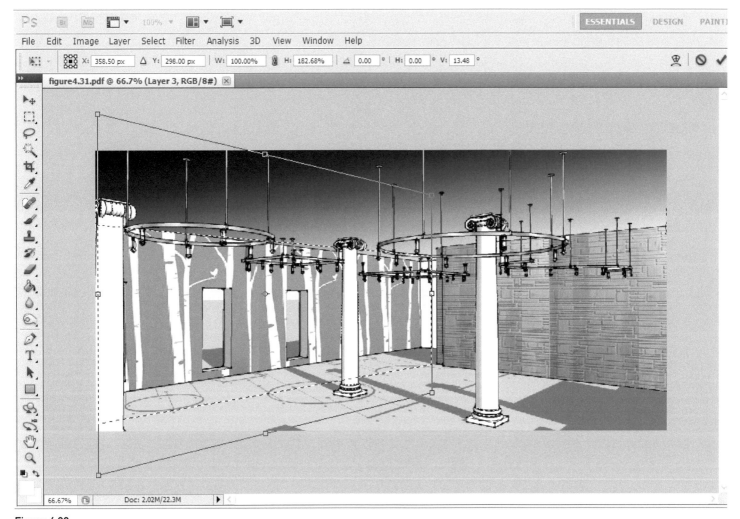

Figure 4.32

Figure 4.33

Figure 4.34

Figure 4.35

15. Bring human figures into your perspective drawing. The method for this is the same as described in the previous chapter. Make sure to create different layers for different objects. Your drawing should look like Figure 4.36.

Applying Materials on the Ceiling in Perspective

Figure 4.37 shows a perspective view that has been modified by Photoshop. The perspective view was originally created in Trimble SketchUp, as shown in Figure 4.38. The stone wall material, wood ceiling, panels, furniture, partition material, and human figures were added in Photoshop.

The procedure for applying material on the ceiling is as follows:

1. Obtain and prepare the ceiling material you are going to use.
2. Open the ceiling material in Photoshop. Use the Rectangular Marquee tool to select the ceiling material. Use Edit > Copy to copy the material, as shown in Figure 4.39.

13. Open an exterior view image in Photoshop. Use the Rectangular Marquee tool to select the image. Go to Edit > Copy to copy the image, as shown in Figure 4.34.
14. Open the perspective drawing in Photoshop. Use the Magic Wand tool to select two windows. Then use Edit > Paste Special > Paste Into to paste the exterior view image. Your drawing should look like Figure 4.35.

Figure 4.36

Figure 4.37

Figure 4.38

3. Open the perspective drawing in Photoshop. Use Edit > Paste Special > Paste Into to paste the ceiling material into the ceiling area, as shown in Figure 4.40.

4. Your drawing should look like Figure 4.41. Note that the ceiling material does not yet match the perspective in the drawing.

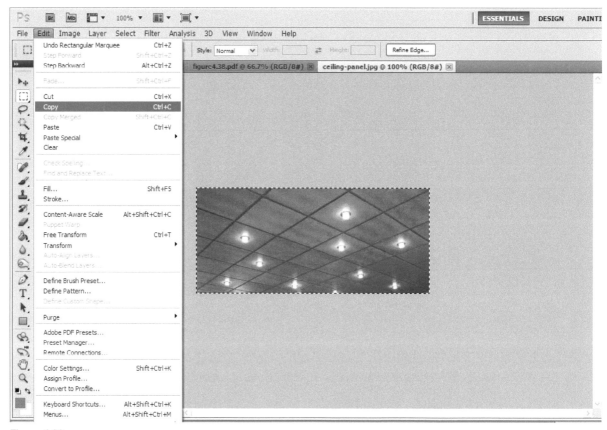

Figure 4.39

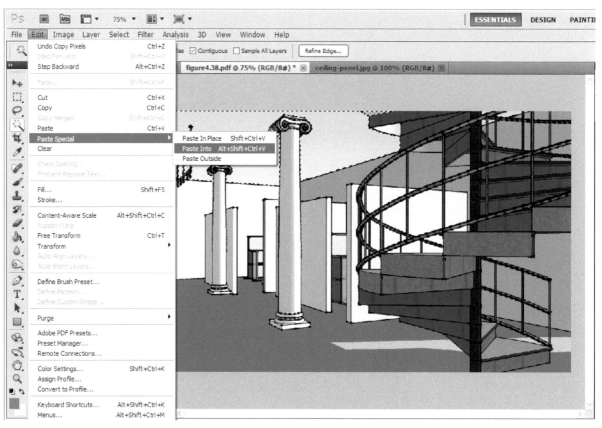

Figure 4.40

5. Use the Rectangular Marquee tool to select the ceiling material. Use Edit >Transform > Distort to adjust the perspective of the ceiling panel to match the perspective in the drawing, shown in Figure 4.42.

6. Drag the small squares to adjust the perspective, as shown in Figure 4.43.

7. After you adjust the perspective to match your drawing, it should look like Figure 4.44.

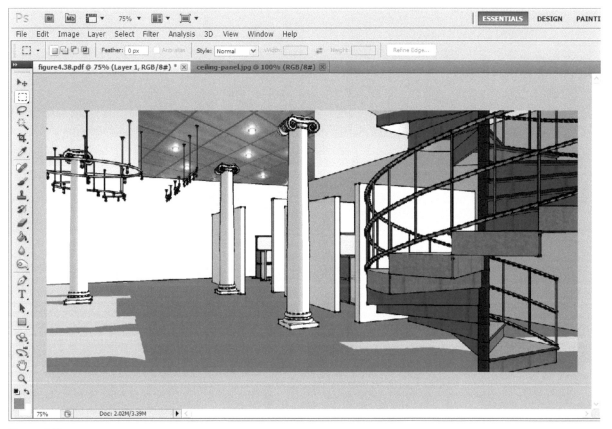

Figure 4.41

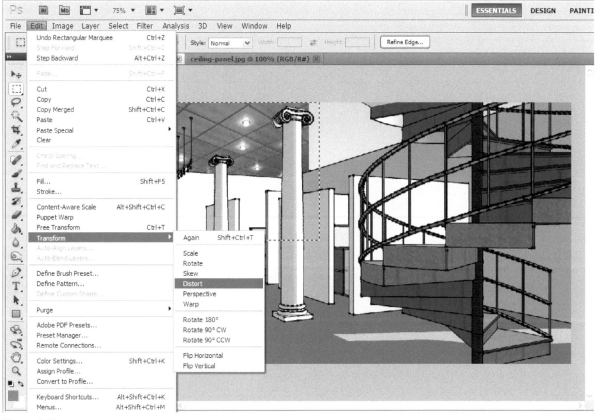

Figure 4.42

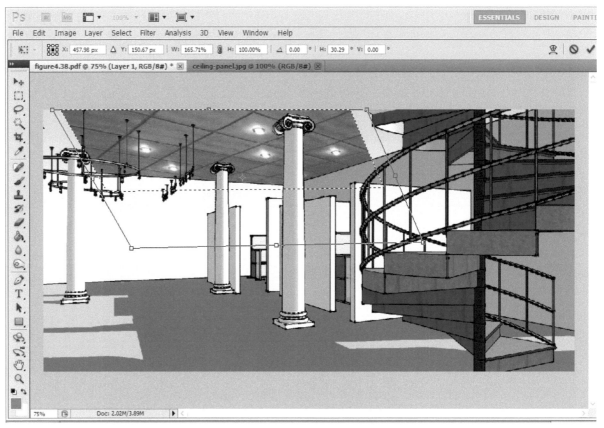

Figure 4.43

Figure 4.44

8. Apply partition panel material to the partition panels. Follow the procedure described earlier in this chapter using the Edit > Paste Special > Paste Into and Edit > Transform > Distort commands. Your drawing should look like Figure 4.45.

9. Apply stone material to the back wall. Follow the procedure described earlier in this chapter using the Edit > Paste Special > Paste Into and Edit > Transform > Perspective commands. Your drawing should look like Figure 4.46.

10. Bring furniture into your perspective drawing. To do this, follow the procedure described in Chapter 3. After bringing in furniture, your drawing should look like Figure 4.47.

11. Add human figures to your perspective drawing. Make sure each object is created on separate layers, as shown in Figure 4.48.

Summary

In this chapter, all perspective drawings were created and enhanced with Photoshop. The rough 3D model was initially created in SketchUp and saved in PDF format. The techniques for using Photoshop to apply materials to enhance and refine perspective were introduced using the following activities:

- Bringing floor material into a perspective drawing
- Applying material to the partition panel
- Applying material on the wall
- Applying material to the ceiling

Key Terms

Edit > Copy
Edit > Paste Special > Paste Into
Edit > Transform > Distort
Edit > Transform > Perspective
Edit > Transform > Scale

Projects

1. Using the perspective provided on the book's companion website http://www.bloomsbury.com/us/photoshop-for-interior-designers-9781609015442/, use Photoshop to add furniture and materials in a perspective drawing. Add human figures to your perspective as well.
2. Use the studio class project you are working on as your initial perspective drawing. Add furniture, materials, and human figures to your perspective drawing.

Figure 4.45

Figure 4.46

Figure 4.47

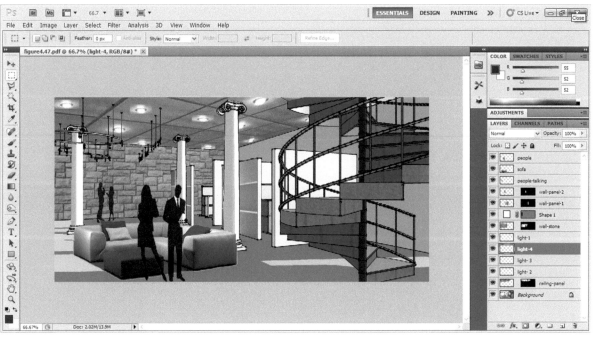

Figure 4.48

5

Working with Lighting

Chapter 5 introduces techniques for applying lighting to drawings using Photoshop. This chapter also explains how to create shadows associated with specific objects. You can add lighting effects to your rendering in the 3D modeling software. However, creating and rendering the perspective with lighting and shadow is time-consuming. This chapter shows a quick way to create lighting and shadow in Photoshop. Demonstrations are given with detailed procedures for applying lighting and creating shadows in perspective drawings. The following demonstrations walk you through adding mixed lightings, creating cast shadows, and creating lighting through stained glass windows.

Note that you must first create a rough raw model in a 3D program. Then you must export your 3D model to TIF, PDF, or JPG format to enhance it in Photoshop.

Using the Lighting Effects Filter

Most **lighting effects** are created through the Lighting Effects filter in Photoshop. To access the **filter**, select Filter > Render > Lighting Effects. This feature offers a fast and photorealistic way of creating an artificial light source. When you first access the Lighting Effects filter, the array of settings and options can seem overwhelming, but the following demonstrations should help you feel more comfortable.

Types of Light

Different preexisting lights are in the Style drop-down box at the top of the Lighting Effects dialogue box. To apply a preexisting light, select the one you want and click OK, as shown in Figure 5.1. Figures 5.2 to 5.18 illustrate the different effects in the interior space from different preexisting lights. The interior space without lighting is shown later in the chapter in Figure 5.31.

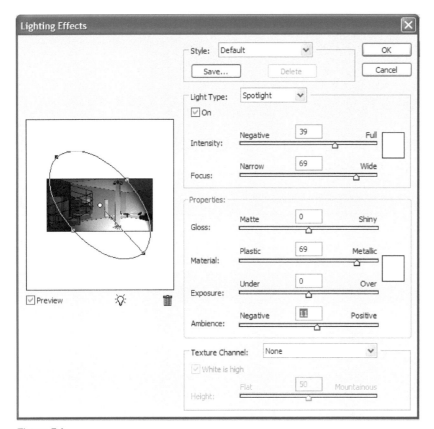

Figure 5.1

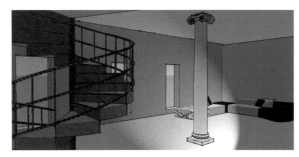

Figure 5.2   Default

Figure 5.3   Soft Omni

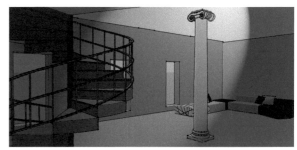

Figure 5.4   2 O'clock Spotlight

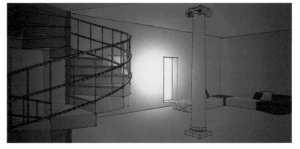

Figure 5.5   Blue Omni

Figure 5.6   Circle of Light

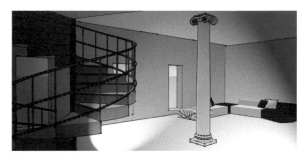

Figure 5.7   Crossing

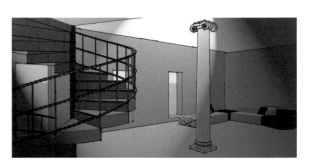

Figure 5.8   Crossing Down

Figure 5.9   Five Lights Down

Figure 5.14   RGB Lights

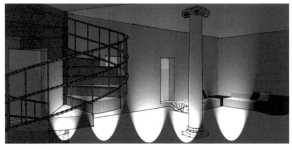

Figure 5.10   Five Lights Up

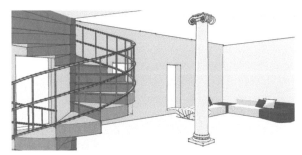

Figure 5.15   Soft Direct Light

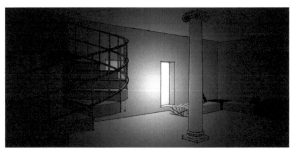

Figure 5.11   Flashlight

Figure 5.16   Soft Spotlight

Figure 5.12   Flood light

Figure 5.17   Three Down

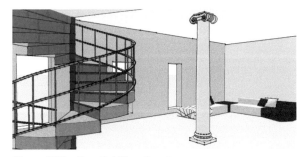

Figure 5.13   Parallel Directional

Figure 5.18   Triple Spotlight

Creating Your Own Lights

Photoshop offers an endless variety of lighting options that allow you to create and customize your own lights beyond the preexisting lighting options.

Light Type

As shown in Figure 5.19, the **Light Type** drop-down box offers three choices:.

- **Directional.** Shines a light from a great distance, such as the way we receive light from the sun, so that the angle of the light does not change. See Figure 5.20.

- **Omni.** Illuminates evenly from a central point in the same way as a light bulb. See Figure 5.21.

- **Spotlight.** Creates an elliptical beam of light that becomes weaker as it travels farther away from the source. See Figure 5.22.

Changing the Light Type Settings

Once you have chosen the light type, you need to position it and define all its parameters. Previous examples in Figures 5.20, 5.21, and 5.22 show elliptical shapes in the dialogue box when you have chosen a type of light. The white circle at the center of the elliptical defines the center point of the light. You use it to reposition the light within the preview window. The light's source is defined by the point that connects to the center of the ellipse by the gray line. To change the ellipse's size and shape, you click and drag the four small squares around the ellipse. If you position the source out of the preview window, then it will not appear in the image, only the light it casts.

The settings are as follows:

- **Intensity.** Regulates how much light emanates from the source. Drag the slider to the right to increase the brightness and to the left to decrease it. See Figure 5.23.

- **Focus.** Defines how much of the ellipse is filled with light. Drag the slider to the right to fill the ellipse and to the left to restrict the spread of light. See Figure 5.23.

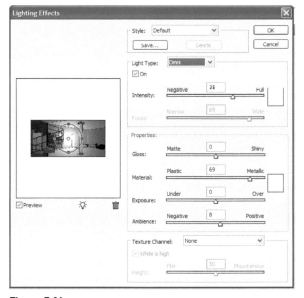

Figure 5.21

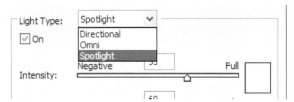

Figure 5.19

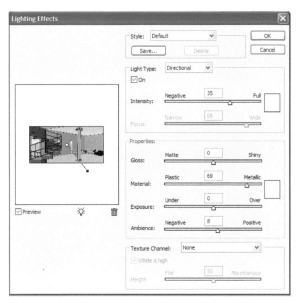

Figure 5.20

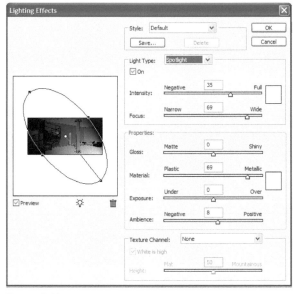

Figure 5.22

- **Light Color.** Creates the effect of a colored filter being placed over a light. Click the white square in the Light Type section, shown in Figure 5.23, to access the Select the Light's Color dialogue box, shown in Figure 5.24. Select the desired color.

Properties

- **Gloss.** Defines how reflective the image should be in terms of the finish of a printed photograph. Drag toward Matte for low reflective and toward Shiny for high reflective properties, as shown in Figure 5.25.

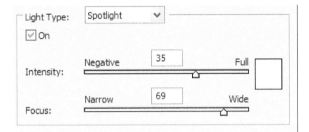

Figure 5.23

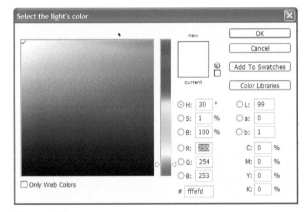

Figure 5.24

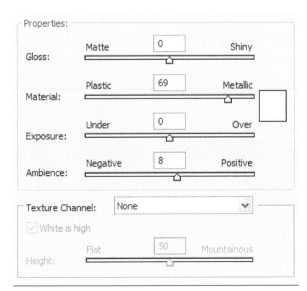

Figure 5.25

- **Material.** Refers to the light's color reflection qualities. Drag toward Plastic if the light's color should be reflected and toward Metallic if the object's color should be reflected. See Figure 5.25.

- **Exposure.** Increases or decreases the overall light in the scene. Drag toward Over to increase light and toward Under to decrease it. See Figure 5.25.

- **Ambience.** Takes into account other light sources in the scene, such as daylight or artificial lights, and diffuses the created light with those light sources. Drag toward Positive to increase light and toward Negative to decrease it. See Figure 5.25.

- **Ambient Light Color.** In the same way as lights can be colored, so can the ambient light in the scene. To change the color, click the white square in the Properties section. See Figure 5.25.

- **Creating Additional Lights.** To create new lights, click and drag from the light bulb icon onto the preview area. A maximum of 16 lights can be created. See Figure 5.26.

- **Duplicating Lights.** Press the Alt key and click and drag from an existing light to duplicate it with exactly the same settings.

- **Deleting Lights.** To remove a light, drag it from its center point into the bin. There must be a minimum of one light left in the scene. See Figure 5.26.

- **Saving New Light Styles.** Having created a lighting setup, you may want to save it for future use with other images. Click the Save button and type a name in the Save dialogue box that appears. The

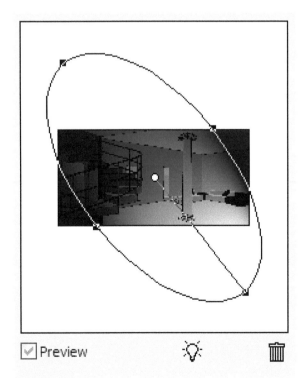

Figure 5.26

Figure 5.27

Figure 5.28

Figure 5.29

Figure 5.30

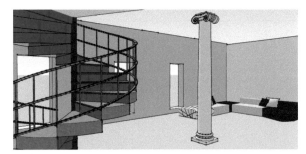

Figure 5.31

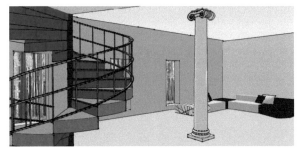

Figure 5.32

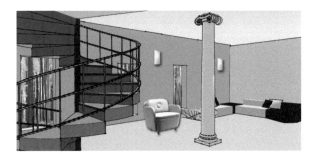

Figure 5.33

Style drop-down box appears as it did with the preexisting lights. See Figure 5.27.

- **Deleting Light Styles.** Select a style and press the Delete button to remove it from Photoshop's folder. See Figure 5.28.

- **Switching Lights On and Off.** For testing purposes, you may want to switch one or more lights off to preview the effect. Select the desired light and uncheck the On box to switch it off. Click again to switch it on. See Figure 5.29.

Mixing Different Types of Light

Figure 5.30 shows an example of applying different types of lights in a perspective drawing that has been refined by Photoshop. The original drawing was created in SketchUp without any lighting (see Figure 5.31). The procedure for applying different types of lights in a perspective drawing is as follows. Once again, you should identify the lighting source before you start adding lighting and shadow in perspective. The lighting effect must be connected to a specific lighting source. Once you have decided on the lighting source, make sure that the lighting effects are consistent. In other words, all the shadows and shade areas are caused by the same lighting source. It is not good practice to show random lighting effects not connected to any planned lighting source.

1. Open the perspective drawing in Photoshop, as shown in Figure 5.31.
2. Bring an exterior view to your perspective drawing. Follow the procedure described in the previous

chapter. Note that you need to use Copy > Paste Into instead of Copy > Paste. Your perspective drawing should now look like Figure 5.32.
3. Bring wall sconces and a chair into your perspective drawing using Edit > Transform > Distort to adjust the perspective. Add **drop shadows** to these objects. Your perspective will look like Figure 5.33.
4. Go to Filter > Render > Lighting Effects to add lights for each wall sconce. The light type is **Flood light**. Drag the small squares to adjust the area that the light will cast. You can also click on the small circle in the center of the ellipse to move the light to a desired location, as shown in Figure 5.34. Then click on the light bulb at the bottom of the dialogue

box and drag the light bulb to the location of the second wall sconce in order to add the second Flood light, as shown in Figure 5.35. After you add two Flood lights to the drawing, your perspective will look like Figure 5.36.

5. Use the Paint Bucket tool to paint the back wall green. Add a framed picture on the green wall. Then go to Filter > Render > Lighting Effects to add a Spotlight on top of the framed picture, as shown in Figure 5.37. Your perspective should now look like Figure 5.38.

6. Create a new layer and use the Gradient Fill tool to add gradient fill in the ceiling area. Go to Filter > Render > Lighting Effects to add one Omni Light to the ceiling area, as shown in Figure 5.39. In the same dialogue box, click on the light bulb

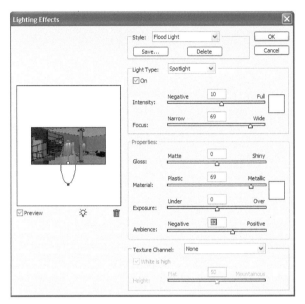

Figure 5.34

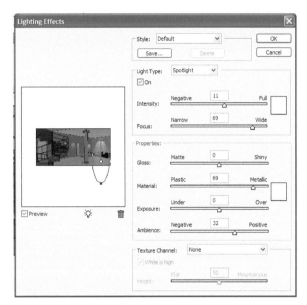

Figure 5.37

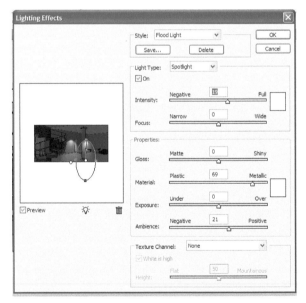

Figure 5.35

Figure 5.38

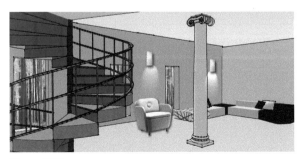

Figure 5.36

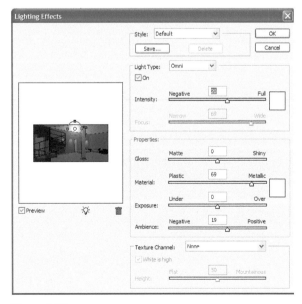

Figure 5.39

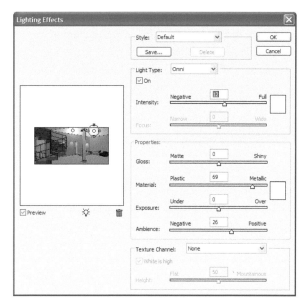

Figure 5.40

Figure 5.41

Figure 5.42

at the bottom of the box and drag it to the desired location for the second Omni light as shown in Figure 5.40. You might need to adjust the intensity. After you add two Omni lights to the ceiling area, your perspective drawing will look like Figure 5.41.

7. Create a new layer called "column-fill" to add gradient fill to the column. Make sure you make the "background" layer active when you use the Magic Wand tool to select the column outline; it will not allow you to select the column outline if you make other layers active. After you select the column outline, make the layer "column-fill" active in order to put the gradient fill on the desired layer. Add two sets of human figures to the drawing, as shown in Figure 5.42.

8. Add shadows for the chair and the column. The procedure is described in the next section.

Creating Cast Shadows

Although Photoshop makes creating drop shadows very easy, the automated process has limitations. In Figure 5.42, the chair and the column are some distance from the wall, so the shadow would appear on the floor. Because of the distance involved, some distortion of the shadow would be apparent. Therefore, a manual technique is used in order to produce a perfectly photographic cast shadow.

1. Create a new layer called "shadow-chair" and another one called "shadow-column." Highlight the "chair" layer and make it active. Use the Rectangular Marquee tool to select the chair as shown in Figure 5.43.

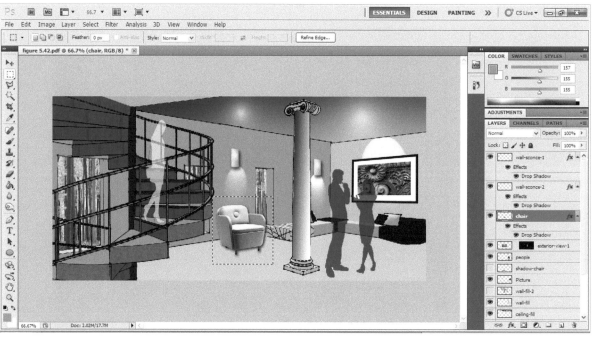

Figure 5.43

Figure 5.44

2. Select Edit > Copy and then Edit > Paste, and paste the chair into the drawing. Use the Magic Wand tool to select the chair. Then go to Select > Modify > Feather. Set the Feather Radius at 10 pixels if you are using a high-resolution file. If you are using a lower-resolution file, set a lower Feather Radius. Save the selection and fill it with a medium gray color, as shown in Figure 5.45. The **Feather** function will make the edge of the shadow a little bit blurry.

3. In the Layer panel, change the **layer blending** mode to **Multiply** and reduce the **Opacity** to 75%. Deselect the current selection and go to Edit > Transform > Distort. Drag the corner squares of the bounding box to adjust the perspective. Press Enter to confirm. See Figure 5.46.

4. The procedure for creating the cast shadow for the column is the same. Make sure the "background" layer is active when you use the Magic Wand tool to select the column outline. After you create shadows

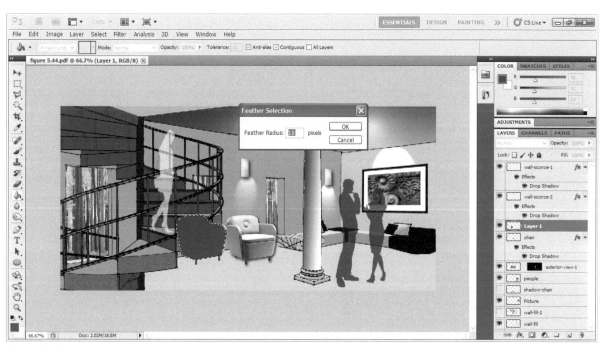

Figure 5.45

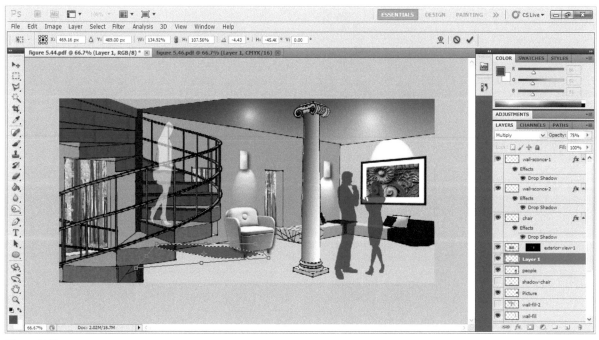

Figure 5.46

Figure 5.47

for both the chair and the column, your perspective should look like Figure 5.47.

Figure 5.48 shows how to create cast shadows from objects. The original perspective, shown in Figure 5.49, was created in SketchUp without any lighting or furniture. After you add lighting, furniture, and human figures, refine the perspective drawing using the following procedure.

1. Open the perspective drawing in Photoshop.
2. Create a new layer, and use the Gradient Fill tool to add gradient fill in the ceiling area. Also add

Figure 5.48

one Omni light in the center of the ceiling area. Bring in travertine floor material to the perspective drawing using Copy > Paste Into. After pasting materials in the floor area, use Edit > Transform > Distort to adjust the perspective of the travertine material See Figure 5.50.
3. Open the JPG file named "window" in Photoshop. Select the window and go to Edit > Copy. Then open the perspective drawing and go to Edit > Paste to paste the window into the drawing. Go to Edit > Transform > Distort to adjust the perspective of the window as shown in Figure 5.51.
4. Add partition patterns to the partition walls, as shown in Figure 5.52. Use Edit > Transform > Distort to make the perspective match the drawing.
5. Add window curtains to the windows. Open the JPG file named "curtain" in Photoshop. Use the Magic Wand tool to select the curtain. Right-click and highlight Select Inverse, as shown in Figure 5.53.
6. Then use Edit > Copy and Edit > Paste to add the curtain. Go to Edit > Transform > Distort to make the curtain perspective match the drawing. Use Edit > Transform > Flip Horizontal to create the left-side curtain. Repeat this procedure to create the curtain

Figure 5.49   **Figure 5.50**

Figure 5.51

Figure 5.52

Figure 5.53

Figure 5.54

Figure 5.55

on the second window. Add drop shadows to all curtains. See Figure 5.54.

7. Bring the piano, the person, and more distant human figures into the perspective. Your drawing should look like Figure 5.55.

8. Make the "Piano" layer active. Use the Rectangular Marquee tool to select the piano. Then use Edit > Copy and Edit > Paste to add the piano into the perspective drawing, as shown in Figure 5.56.

Figure 5.56

9. Rename layer 1 "piano." Use the Magic Wand tool to select the piano. Then use the Paint Bucket tool to fill in the gray color. Make another layer named "shadow-piano." Multiply and change the Opacity to 60%–70%, as shown in Figure 5.57.

10. Select the gray piano. Use Edit > Transform > Distort to make the shadow match the perspective. See Figure 5.58.

11. Repeat the same process to create the cast shadow for the person. After the shadows are created, your perspective should look like Figure 5.59.

Figure 5.57

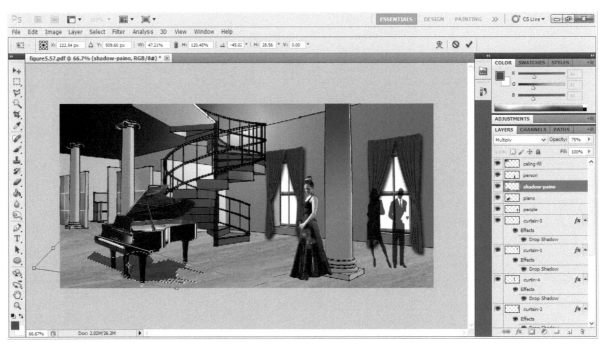

Figure 5.58

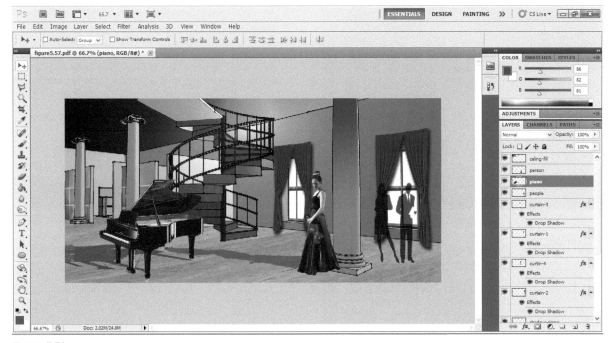

Figure 5.59

Cast Light through Windows

A light source can often add visual drama to a scene. Lighting can be used as one of the design elements in an interior space. Interior designers and architects use lighting in their designs in order to achieve special effects.

Figure 5.60 shows how to create cast light through a window. The design intent is to add a hint of the Arts and Crafts style in the interior space; stained glass windows as well as Arts and Crafts–style wall sconces have therefore been added to the design. The original perspective was created in SketchUp.

1. Open the perspective drawing shown in Figure 5.61 in Photoshop.
2. Add gradient fill to the ceiling area, and add one Omni light in the center of the ceiling area. Bring stained glass windows as well as Arts and Crafts–style wall sconces into the drawing. Add Flood lights for each wall sconce and add drop shadows to each wall sconce. See Figure 5.62.
3. Add gradient fill to the column. Bring in a framed picture to the wall. Also add gray color to the floor area (see Figure 5.63).
4. Apply stone material on the wall. Use Edit > Transform > Perspective and Edit > Transform > Distort to match the perspective in the drawing. To tone down the stone wall, use the Paint Bucket tool to fill in gray color on top of the stone wall. But make sure that the layer Opacity is set to 30%–40%. Add drop shadows to the stone wall. See Figure 5.64.

Figure 5.60

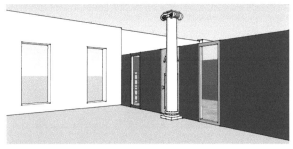

Figure 5.61

Figure 5.62

Figure 5.63

Figure 5.64

5. Select the stained glass window, using the **Polygon Lasso tool** and following the perspective of the window shown in Figure 5.65.

6. Use Edit > Copy and Edit > Paste to add the stained glass window onto a new layer named "window-1." Go to **Edit > Transform > Flip Vertical** to turn the duplicated window image upside down. See Figure 5.66.

7. Use Edit > Transform > Distort to adjust the perspective of the stained glass on the floor. Make sure that the perspective matches the drawing perspective. See Figure 5.67.

8. To give the stained glass image more of an airy feel, change the layer blending mode to Screen, as shown in Figure 5.68.

9. The window is not a perfect optical device (as, say, a projector lens would be), so we would expect it to be vague, stretched, and distorted rather than crisp. To create this, click **Filter > Blur > Motion Blur**, and set the Angle to 0 and the Distance to 19, as shown in Figure 5.69.

Figure 5.65   **Figure 5.66**   **Figure 5.67**

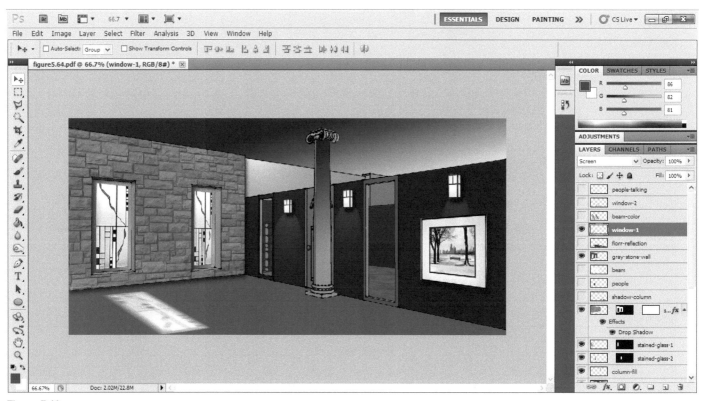

Figure 5.68

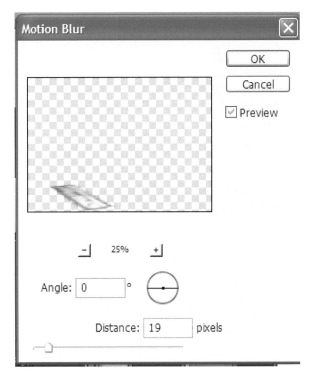

Figure 5.69

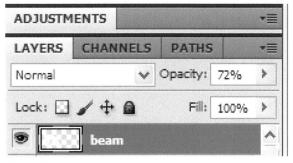

Figure 5.70

10. For a really dynamic feel, create the beam of light being cast through the window onto the floor. First, create a new layer called "Beam" and set the layer Opacity to 60–70%, as shown in Figure 5.70.

11. Using the Polygon Lasso tool, create the perimeter of the light beam from the window to the floor as shown in Figure 5.71 Then click Select > Modify > Feather and set the Feather Radius to 10 pixels, as shown in the figure.

12. Set up the Gradient tool Foreground to Transparent linear option, making sure that white is the foreground color. Drag a gradient from top (upper left) to the bottom (lower right). This creates a soft flood of white that fades out subtly. Repeat for the second window. See Figure 5.72.

13. Since the window has colored glass, light being transmitted through it should hint of colors. Create a new layer called "beam-color" and set the Opacity to 7%.

14. Select the Gradient tool and choose the Transparent Rainbow linear gradient option (the second from the left on the last row). This gradient is part of the default gradient set. See Figure 5.73.

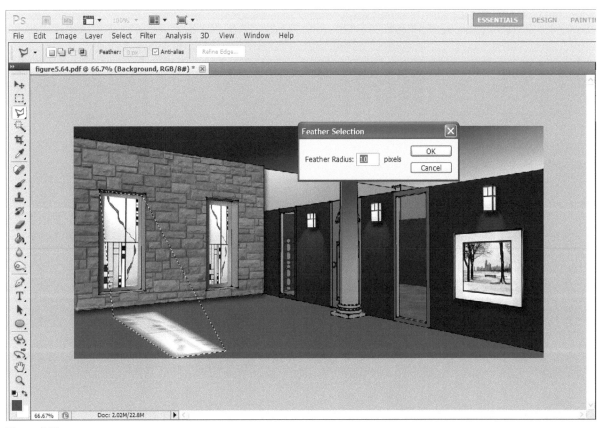

Figure 5.71

Figure 5.72

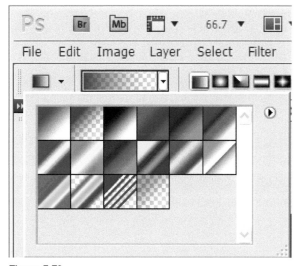

Figure 5.73

15. Drag the gradient across the beam from the lower left corner to the upper right corner. The idea is to create just the suggestion of colored light.

16. To add a few subtle streaks to the colored light, change the layer's blend mode to Pin Light, as shown in Figure 5.74.

Shadows and Reflection

Finally, a highly polished floor will give the illusion of the window image being projected onto the floor. You can achieve this effect by creating a subtle reflection of the side wall:

1. Using the Polygon Lasso tool, outline the images you want to copy. Highlight all the layers that contain the objects you are going to copy. In this case, copy the framed picture and three wall sconces as well as the background layer. Go to **Edit > Copy Merged**, as shown in Figure 5.75.

2. Paste the side wall onto the perspective. Use Edit > Transform > Flip Vertical to make the side wall upside down, as shown in Figure 5.76.

3. Rename the layer "floor-reflection" and make it active. Use the Rectangular Marquee tool to select the flipped wall. Go to Edit > Transform > Distort to make the wall perspective match the drawing perspective, as shown in Figure 5.77.

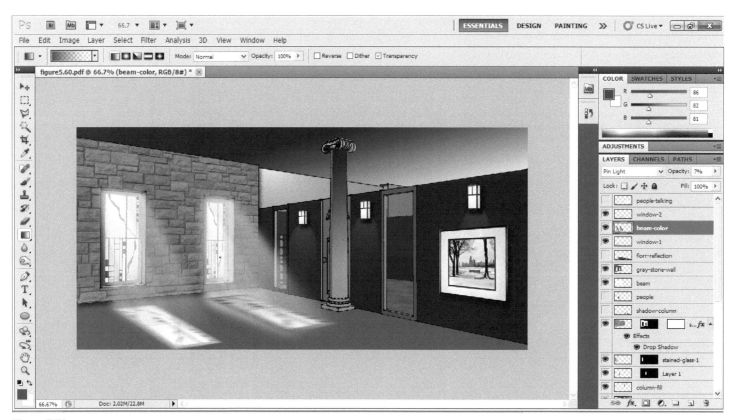

Figure 5.74

Figure 5.75

Figure 5.76

Figure 5.77

SHADOWS AND REFLECTION 93

Figure 5.78

cast lighting for stained glass windows. In addition, creating floor reflections was described.

Specifically, the following techniques were discussed:

- Applying mixed lighting types in an interior space
- Creating cast shadows for objects
- Creating cast shadows for stained glass windows
- Creating floor reflections

Key Terms

Ambience
Ambient light color
Creating additional lights
Deleting lights
Deleting light styles
Directional
Drop shadows
Duplicating lights
Edit > Copy Merged
Edit > Transform > Flip Vertical
Exposure
Feather
Filter
Filter > Blur > Motion Blur
Flood Light
Focus
Gloss
Intensity

4. Rename the layer "floor-reflection." Set the Opacity at 15% and the select the Pin Light layer blend. Make the "beam" and "color-beam" layers active, as shown in Figure 5.78.
5. Add human figures and column shadows to the drawing. Your perspective should look like Figure 5.79.

Summary

In this chapter, basic techniques of applying lighting to perspective drawings were introduced. The chapter started with a discussion of the Lighting Effects filter in Photoshop. Then more advanced techniques were demonstrated, including applying mixed lighting in interior space, creating cast shadows for the objects, and creating

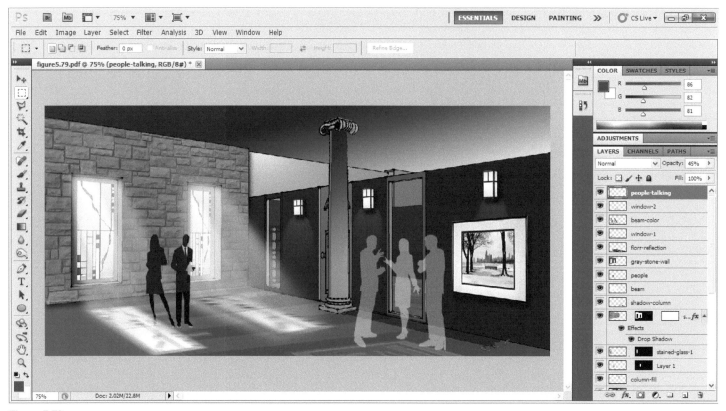

Figure 5.79

Layer blending
Light Color
Light Type
Lighting effects
Material
Multiply layer blending mode
Omni
Opacity
Pin Light layer blending mode
Polygon Lasso tool
Saving new light styles
Screen layer blending mode
Spotlight
Switching lights on and off

Projects

1. Using the perspective provided on the book's companion website http://www.bloomsbury.com/us/photoshop-for-interior-designers-9781609015442/, create mixed lighting effects in a perspective drawing in Photoshop. Add human figures to your perspective as well.

2. Use the studio class project you are working on as your initial perspective drawing. Create lighting effects and cast shadows in the perspective drawing.

3. Create cast lighting for the stained glass window using the perspective provided on the book's companion website. You can create the style you prefer for this interior space.

6

Special Effects in Photoshop

Chapter 6 introduces techniques of using special effects, such as the **watercolor effect,** oil **pastel effect,** and **pencil sketch effect** via the Filter feature of Photoshop in order to communicate design intent more effectively. For example, a **sepia** or brown-toned image is often used for artistic effect or to simulate an old-time look. These effects also add a human touch to often cold- and sterile-looking computer-generated drawings. In presentation drawings, sometimes a combination of different drawings, such as a watercolor or sepia rendering combined with a digital rendering, presents a unique style to convey the design intent. Refer back to Figure 1.1 for an example.

Creating Sepia from a Black-and-White or Color Image

The Filter feature in Photoshop allows you to create sepia or brown-toned images easily. You can start with a black-and-white (grayscale) or a color image. Figure 6.1 is a sepia image that was created from Figure 6.2, a color image.

Several different methods for creating a sepia image are available, none of which is inherently better than the others. The choice is at the designer's discretion and the needs of the project. The following demonstrates a simple step-by-step procedure for creating a sepia image.

1. Open Figure 6.2 in Photoshop.
2. Select Image > Mode > Grayscale to change the image to grayscale, as shown in Figure 6.3.
3. Go back to Mode in the top menu and select **RGB Color,** as shown in Figure 6.4. Note: If you skip this step, you will not be able to change the color of a grayscale image.
4. Next, to create a new Color Balance layer for your image, select Layer > New Adjustment Layer > Color Balance, as shown in Figure 6.5. If Color Balance is grayed out in the menu, it usually means the image needs to be changed back to RGB from Grayscale in the previous step.

Figure 6.1

Figure 6.2

Figure 6.3

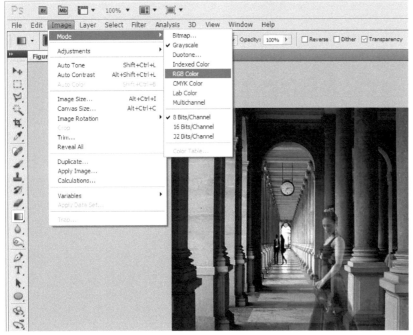

Figure 6.4

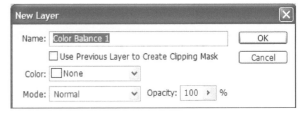

Figure 6.6

5. A dialogue box appears, as shown in Figure 6.6. Click OK.

6. The Color Balance Adjustments dialogue box appears on the right side of the screen. Adjust the slider to change the value under Shadows, Midtones, and Highlights, as shown in Figure 6.7. Sepia usually consists of red and yellow. As a starting point, try setting the Shadows feature to (+20, 0, –5) in the Color Balance Adjustments dialogue box shown in Figure 6.7. Click Midtones and select (+30, 0, –25). Set Highlights to (+10, 0, –5). You can change the values as desired.

7. Click Layers at the bottom of Color Balance Adjustments on the right side of the screen. Note that the new layer, Color Balance, has been added to the layer list, as shown in Figure 6.8.

Photoshop provides different options to accomplish the same result. You can also create sepia images using a different method. The second method for creating sepia images is to open the color image in Photoshop and select Image > Adjustments > Desaturate to change the color image to a black-and-white image. Since the image was not converted to grayscale, it is still in RGB mode, and there is no need to convert the mode back as described in the first method. Add a Color Balance layer (as described in the previous method) and adjust the settings to obtain the desired result.

Creating Hand-Colored Sepia

Sepia already makes the image look a bit old-fashioned. A soft pastel coloring will enhance the effect and is often even more appropriate for an old-time effect. Figures 6.9 to 6.12 are sepia images with soft pastel-like color.

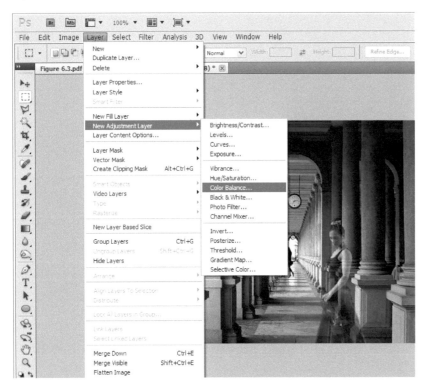

Figure 6.5

Figure 6.7

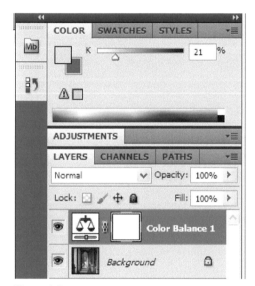

Figure 6.8

Figure 6.9

Figure 6.10

Figure 6.11

Figure 6.12

The following procedure shows how to create a sepia image with a hand-colored look more quickly than having to do the actual hand painting. Because designers must often accomplish tasks on tight schedules, this method is invaluable.

1. Open the color image in Photoshop (see Figure 6.2), and then create a "Hue/Saturation" layer (Layer > New Adjustment Layer > Hue/Saturation). A dialogue box appears, as shown in Figure 6.13. Click OK.

2. The Hue/Saturation dialogue box appears on the right side of the screen. Move the saturation slider to the left to remove the color in the image, as shown in Figure 6.14. The color image becomes a black-and-white image.

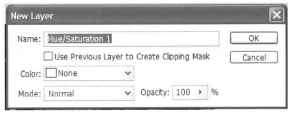

Figure 6.13

3. Now create a new "Color Balance" layer (Layer > New Adjustment Layer > Color Balance). Adjust the Shadows (+20, 0, −5), Midtones (+30, 0, −25), and Highlights (+10, 0, −5) to a pleasing value of sepia. The values shown in Figure 6.15 are good starting points.

4. Place the cursor on the bottom in the Layers panel. If it is not shown, open it by selecting Window > Layers. Duplicate the "Background" layer (right-click and highlight Duplicate Layer). Drag the duplicate layer so that it is at the top of the stack of layers, as shown in Figure 6.16. After you drag the duplicated layer to the top, your image will be color. You also can duplicate the "Background" layer at the beginning and turn off the original "Background" layer. Then create a "Hue/Saturation" layer and a "Color Balance" layer, and adjust the Shadows, Midtones, and Highlights values.

5. Highlight the "Background Copy" layer, adjusting the opacity as shown in Figure 6.17. Here a value of 35% was chosen, which still shows the sepia tone but allows a bit of the color to show through. This provides a pastel look to the colors and keeps them looking old-fashioned.

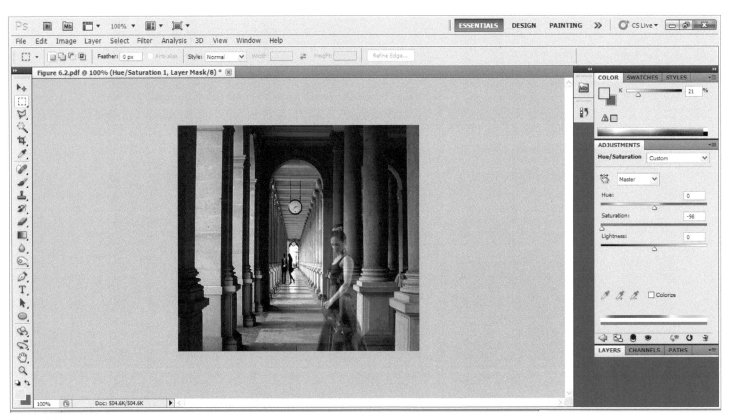

Figure 6.14

Figure 6.15

Figure 6.16

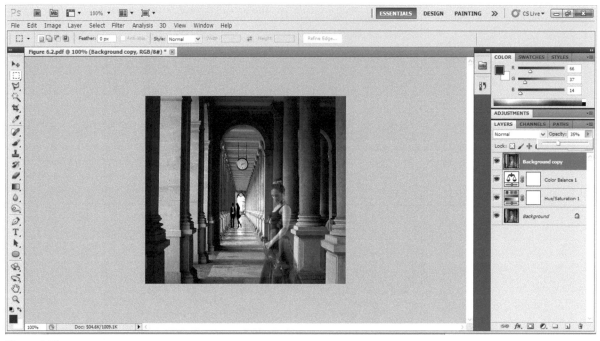

Figure 6.17

Since it conveys a sense of time in the distant past, sepia is frequently used to present historical architecture. The following is another example of creating sepia images that presents the floor plan of the Pantheon in Rome. The Pantheon is one of the oldest buildings in architectural history and sepia is an effective and appropriate tone to represent this building.

1. Open the black-and-white Pantheon floor plan in Photoshop. Be sure to set the mode back to RGB by selecting Image > Mode > RGB Color.
2. Create a new "Color Balance" layer by going to Layer > New Adjustment Layer, as shown in Figure 6.18.

3. In the Adjustments dialogue box, set Shadows as (+20, 0, –5), Midtones as (+30, 0, –25), and Highlights as (+10, 0, –5). The result is a sepia floor plan as shown in Figure 6.19.
4. Use the Gradient tool to add sepia color to the rest of the floor plan as shown in Figure 6.20.

Creating a Watercolor Effect

Watercolor provides a free and abstract quality to a drawing and is an artistic medium favored by many designers. With the Watercolor filter in Photoshop, you can create a watercolor effect very quickly. Figures 6.21 to 6.23 are examples of watercolor effect. Figure 6.21 is a hand-colored sepia with watercolor effect.

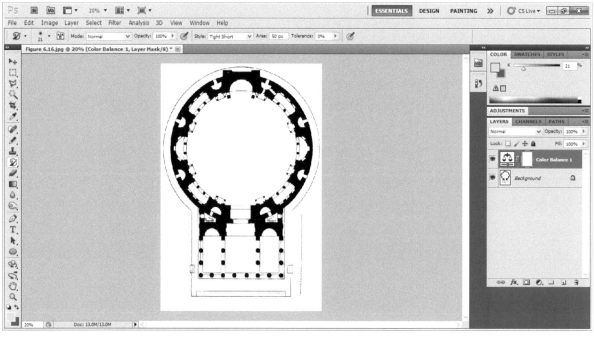

Figure 6.18

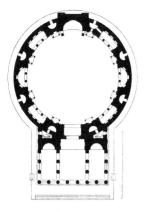

Figure 6.19   Figure 6.20

Figure 6.21

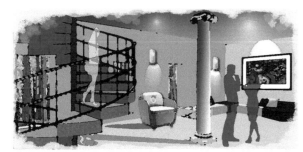

Figure 6.22

Figure 6.23

The procedure for applying a watercolor effect is very simple and straightforward.

1. Open Figure 6.11 in Photoshop. Before you create a watercolor effect, flatten the image so that the effect is applied to all the layers, not just the active one. Flattening the image combines all the layers into one. Select Layer > Flatten Image, as shown in Figure 6.24.
2. After flattening the image, you will only see one layer, called "Background," on the right side of the screen. Select Filter > Artistic > Watercolor, as shown in Figure 6.25.
3. You will then be prompted by a preview screen as shown in Figure 6.26. Click on + or – at the lower left corner to zoom in or zoom out on the image.
4. Click OK. The image appears with the watercolor effect. To make the drawing look like a real hand-drawn watercolor, you must give it a soft edge for a brushed effect. To achieve this, use the Brush tool in Photoshop. The Brush tool can be accessed on the left side of the screen, as shown in Figure 6.27.

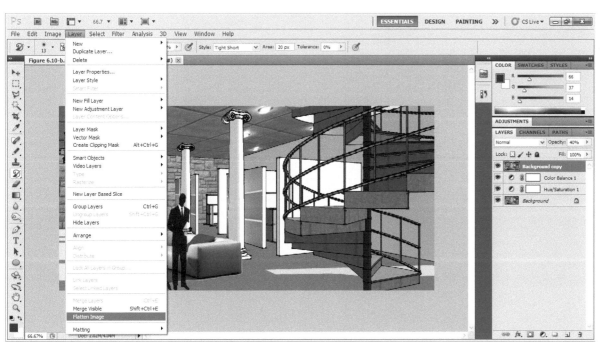

Figure 6.24

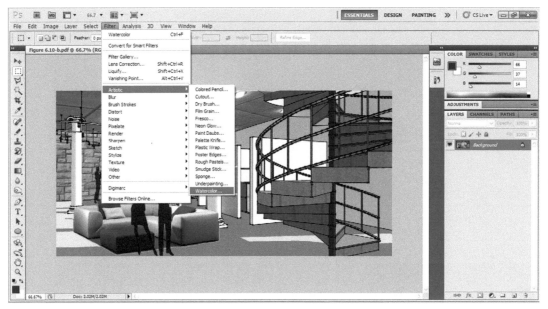

Figure 6.25

Figure 6.26

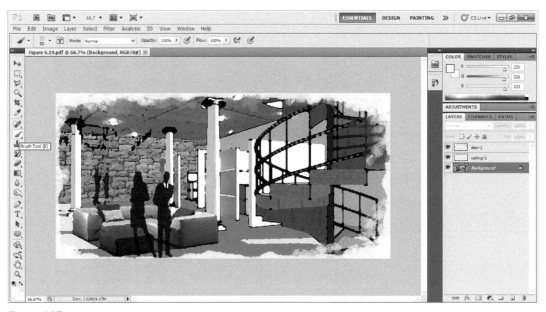

Figure 6.27

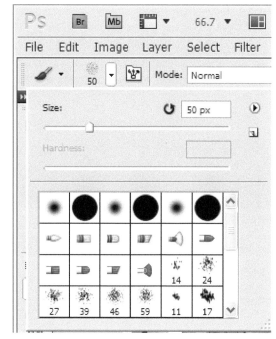

Figure 6.28

Figure 6.29

Figure 6.30

5. You also can change the brush type and size. Click on the small drop-down menu on the left side at the top of the screen as shown in Figure 6.28.

6. You can also soften the edge by using different colors and different layer opacity. In Figure 6.21, two new layers were created. The first step is to use the Brush tool to draw some free brush strokes around the drawing using white color. Make sure your foreground color is white (see Figure 6.29).

7. Create a new layer called "ceiling-1." Use the Brush tool to draw some brush strokes using a lighter brown color. Select your foreground color as light brown in order to soften the transition for the brown ceiling edge. Set layer "ceiling-1" opacity at 78% (see Figure 6.30).

8. Create another new layer called "stair-2." Use the Brush tool to draw some brush strokes in the staircase area in order to create a soft transition for the edge in the staircase area. Use warm gray as foreground, and set layer opacity at 76%, as shown in Figure 6.31.

Figures 6.22 and 6.23 were created using the same process.

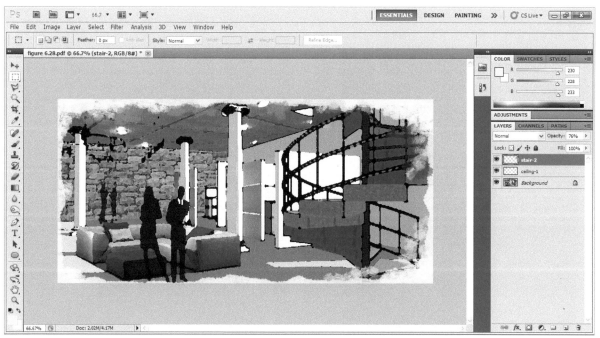

Figure 6.31

Creating a Pastel Effect

In Photoshop, you also can create a drawing that looks like a pastel. The technique is very simple and straightforward. Figures 6.32 and 6.33 are two examples of pastel drawings that were created using the Pastel Artistic filter.

1. Open the original drawing in Photoshop. Flatten the image by selecting Layer > Flatten Image. Go to Filter > Artistic > Rough Pastels, as shown in Figure 6.34.

2. The preview screen shown in Figure 6.35 appears. Click + or – at the lower left corner to zoom in or out of the image.

Figure 6.32

Figure 6.33

Figure 6.34

Figure 6.35

3. Click OK. The image now appears with a pastel effect. To make the drawing look like a real, hand-drawn pastel, create a soft edge by using the Brush tool. This tool can be accessed on the left side of the screen, as shown in Figure 6.27.

4. You also can change the brush type and size. Click on the small drop-down menu on the left side at the top of your screen, as shown in Figure 6.28.

5. Use different colors and a different layer opacity to soften the edge. First create a new layer, as was shown in Figure 6.32. Then use the Brush tool to draw some loose, free brush strokes around the drawing in a light gray color. Make sure your foreground color is light gray (see Figure 6.36).

6. Next, create a new layer called "ceiling-1." Use the Brush tool to draw some brush strokes using light gray color—lighter than the first light gray. Select your foreground color as light gray in order to soften the transition for the brown ceiling edge. Set layer "ceiling-1" opacity at 78%, as shown in Figure 6.37.

Note: Figure 6.33 was created using the same process.

Creating Other Special Effects

In addition to the watercolor effect and pastel effect, you can use Photoshop's Filter Gallery to create many other special effects. Following is an overview of them.

Photoshop Artistic Filters

The filters in the **Artistic category** allow the designer to achieve effects of hand-rendered drawings. Figures 6.26 and 6.35 show the Artistic filter effects available. The following are examples of these special effects in drawings and are more appropriate for interior architectural

Figure 6.36

Figure 6.37

drawings. Others may be more appropriate for other types of artistic expression. Access the Artistic dialogue box by selecting Filter > Filter Gallery.

Cutout

Select **Cutout** as shown in Figure 6.38. Use + and − to zoom in or zoom out on your image. You also can adjust Number of Levels, Edge Simplicity, and Edge Fidelity

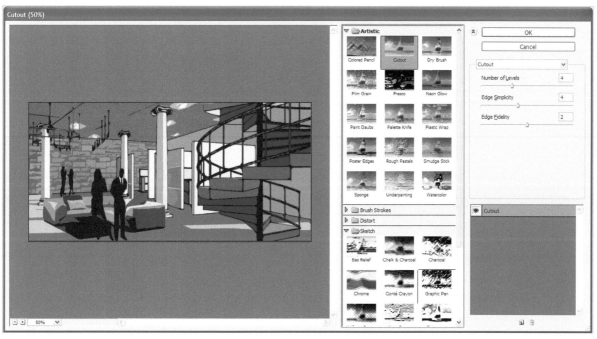

Figure 6.38

Figure 6.39

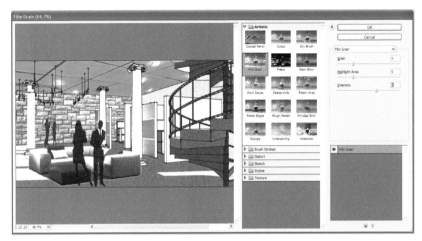

Figure 6.40

Figure 6.41

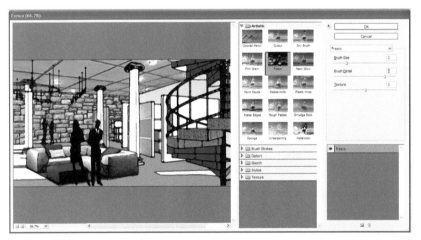

Figure 6.42

Figure 6.43

to achieve the desired effect. The current values for these parameters are 4, 4, 2. Your drawing will look like Figure 6.39.

Film Grain

Select **Film Grain** as shown in Figure 6.40. Use + and – to zoom in or out on your image. You also can adjust Grain, Highlight Area, and Intensity to achieve the desired effect. The current values for these parameters are (5, 5, 6), as shown in Figure 6.40. Click OK. Your drawing will look like Figure 6.41.

Fresco

Select **Fresco** as shown in Figure 6.42. Use + and – to zoom in or out on your image. You also can adjust Brush Size, Brush Detail, and Texture to achieve the desired effect. The current values for these parameters are (2, 8, 2), as shown in Figure 6.42. Click OK. Your drawing will look like Figure 6.43.

Poster Edges

Select **Poster Edges**, as shown in Figure 6.44. Use + and – to zoom in or out on your image. You also can adjust Edge Thickness, Edge Intensity, and Posterization to achieve the desired effect. The current values for these parameters are (2, 5, 4), as shown in Figure 6.44. Click OK. Your drawing will look like Figure 6.45.

Smudge Stick

Select **Smudge Stick,** as shown in Figure 6.46. Use + and – to zoom in or out on your image. You also can adjust Stroke Length, Highlight Area, and Intensity to achieve the desired effect. The current values for these parameters are (2, 4, 6), as shown in Figure 6.46. Click OK. Your drawing will look like Figure 6.47.

Brush Strokes Filter

In addition to the Artistic category in Photoshop is a category called **Brush Strokes.** It is listed just below the Artistic category as shown in Figure 6.48. There are eight different special effects, but the **Ink Outlines** option is more appropriate for use in interior architectural drawings.

Ink Outlines

Select **Ink Outlines** as shown in Figure 6.48. Use + and – to zoom in or out on your image. You also can adjust Stroke Length, Dark Intensity, and Light Intensity to achieve a desired effect. The current values for these parameters are (3, 7, 15) as shown in Figure 6.48. Click OK. Your drawing will look like Figure 6.49.

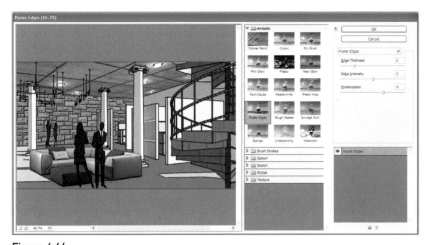

Figure 6.44

Figure 6.45

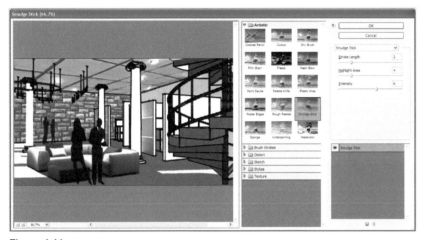

Figure 6.46

Figure 6.47

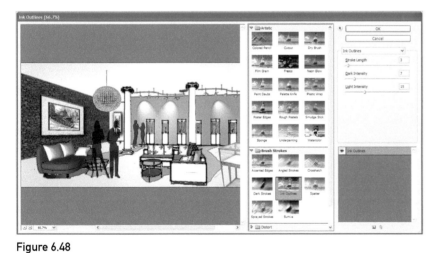

Figure 6.48

Figure 6.49

Sketch Filter

In addition to the Artistic and Brush Strokes categories in Photoshop is a category called **Sketch**. It is listed just below the Brush Strokes category, as shown in Figure 6.50. There are 14 different special effects, but **Graphic Pen** is more appropriate for use in interior architectural drawings.

Graphic Pen

Select **Graphic Pen,** as shown in Figure 6.50. Use + and – to zoom in or out on your image. You also can adjust Stroke Length and Light/Dark Balance to achieve the desired effect. The current values for these parameters are (8, 71), as shown in Figure 6.50. Select Stroke Direction as Right Diagonal. Click OK. Your drawing will look like Figure 6.51.

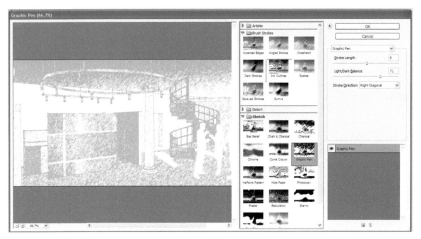

Figure 6.50

Figure 6.51

Figure 6.52

You will also need to select Image > Adjustments > Brightness/Contrast to darken the drawing and increase the contrast. After adjusting the darkness and contrast, your drawing will look like Figure 6.52.

Texture Filter

Another category of filters is called **Texture.** It is listed just below the Sketch and Style categories, as shown in Figure 6.53. There are six different special effects, but **Grain** and **Texturizer** are more appropriate for interior architectural drawing use.

Grain

Select **Grain,** as shown in Figure 6.53. Use + and – to zoom in or out on your image. You also can adjust Intensity and Contrast to achieve a desired effect. The current values for these parameters are (40, 60), as shown in Figure 6.53. Select Grain Type as Regular. Click OK. Your drawing will look like Figure 6.54.

You also can use the Grain effect to make the watercolor effect more realistic. Open the watercolor effect drawing, shown in Figure 6.22, in Photoshop. Select Grain, as shown in Figure 6.55. Use + and – to zoom in or out on your image. The current values for these

parameters are (40, 60), as shown in Figure 6.55. Select Grain Type as Enlarged. Click OK. Your drawing will look like Figure 6.56.

The following are two drawings that have been modified by using Grain. Figure 6.57 uses Regular Grain and Figure 6.58 uses Enlarged grain. Both give the drawing a sense of watercolor paper texture. You decide which option would be best for your drawings.

Texturizer

Select **Texturizer,** as shown in Figure 6.59. Use + and – to zoom in or out on your image. For Texture, select Canvas. Then set Scaling at 145% and Relief at 5. From the drop-down menu, set Light as Top Right, as shown in Figure 6.59. This is a starting point; you can adjust these parameters to achieve the desired effect. Click OK. Your drawing will look like Figure 6.60. The drawing now looks more like an oil pastel drawing. Figure 6.61 was created using the same process.

Figure 6.53

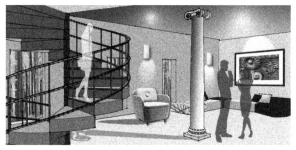

Figure 6.54

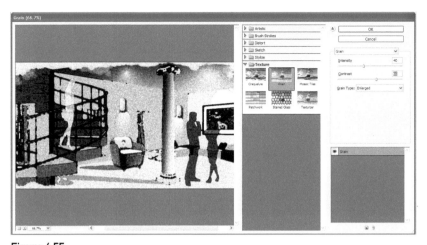

Figure 6.55

Figure 6.56

Figure 6.57

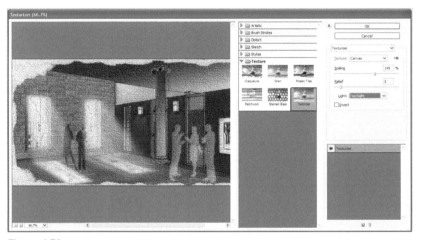

Figure 6.58

Figure 6.59

Figure 6.60

Figure 6.61

Summary

This chapter introduced techniques of creating special effects by using Photoshop to achieve various artistic effects. The following effects were presented and demonstrated:

- Creating sepia and sepia with pastel color to convey an old-time effect

- Creating a watercolor effect in a drawing to add a sense of looseness and human touch to the drawing

- Creating a pastel effect in a drawing to add a hand-rendered quality

- Using the Cutout filter

- Using the Film Grain filter

- Using the Fresco filter

- Using the Poster Edges filter

- Using the Smudge Stick filter

- Using the Ink Outlines filter

- Using the Graphic Pen filter

- Using the Grain filter

- Using the Texturizer filter

Key Terms

Artistic category
Brush Strokes
Cutout
Film Grain
Fresco
Grain
Graphic Pen

Ink Outlines
Pastel effect
Pencil sketch effect
Poster Edges
Sepia
Sketch category
Smudge Stick
Texture
Texturizer
Watercolor effect

Projects

1. Add a sepia tone with color effect to the drawings you created in the exercises in Chapter 5.
2. Add watercolor and pastel effects to the drawing created in the previous chapter.
3. Using your studio project drawings, create your choice of special effects, such as fresco, poster edge, cutout.
4. Using watercolor drawing and pastel, add texture to your drawing to present the effect of watercolor on paper and canvas.

7

Adding Entourage

Chapter 7 introduces techniques for adding entourage to drawings. Entourage usually includes people, trees, and vehicles. Entourage provides a sense of scale, adds interest, and conveys the atmosphere of the space presented. Therefore, successfully adding entourage to drawings will make them more appealing.

Adding People and Trees to a Drawing

Figure 7.1 was created in Trimble SketchUp. In addition to floor material, artwork on the wall, and gray color on the ceiling and wall, human figures and a tree were also added, as shown in Figure 7.2. The entourage shows a sense of scale and provides a sense of atmosphere. The following demonstrates the step-by-step procedure for adding people and trees to the drawing.

1. Open your perspective (see Figure 7.1) in Photoshop.
2. Use the **Gradient Fill tool** to add gray color to the ceiling area and on the wall in order to create different values and contrast. You also can bring in an exterior view to the drawing, as shown in Figure 7.3.

3. Add wood floor material to the drawing. You can use Edit > Transform > Distort to adjust the perspective of the floor material. Add framed pictures to the drawing as well. You can use Edit > Transform > Perspective to make the framed pictures match your drawing perspective. Use Drop Shadow to add shadows to the framed pictures, as shown in Figure 7.4.
4. Bring people and a tree to the drawing, as shown in Figure 7.5. If the background of the entourage photo is white, it is easy to copy the entourage to your drawing. First use the Magic Wand tool to click on the background; then right-click and choose Select Inverse. This selects only the entourage and not the background. Copy and paste the entourage into your drawing, as demonstrated in previous chapters.

Figure 7.1

Figure 7.4

Figure 7.2

Figure 7.5

Figure 7.3

5. If your photo has a background like the one shown in Figure 7.6, you must first eliminate it before copying and pasting. To do so, select the **Polygonal Lasso tool** to trace the edge of the two people, as shown in Figure 7.7.

6. Now use the Magic Wand tool and click on the background. Choose Select > Inverse to select the two people without the background (Figure 7.8). Then go to Edit > Copy and Edit > Paste to add them to a new drawing, as shown in Figure 7.9.

7. To add a tree to your drawing, open the tree photo and follow the instructions in Step 6. See Figures 7.10 and 7.11.

Figure 7.6

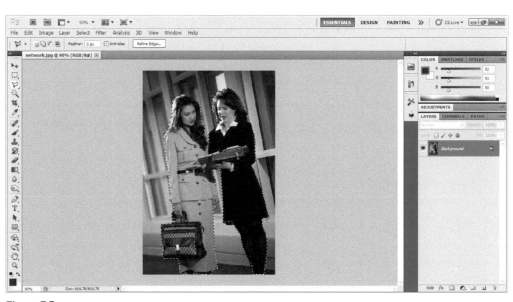

Figure 7.7

Figure 7.8

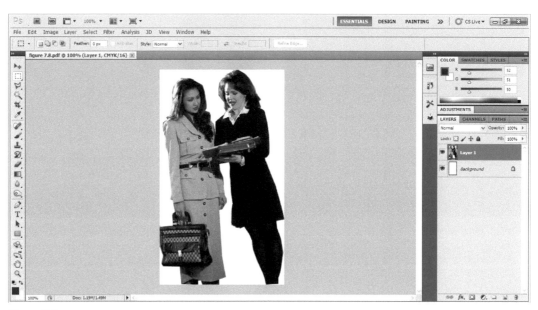

Figure 7.9

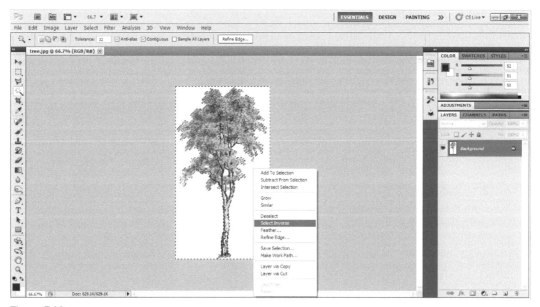

Figure 7.10

Figure 7.11

Adding Shadows to Entourage

After bringing the entourage to your perspective drawing, you can add shadows. To create shadows for the tree and human figures, follow these steps:

1. Open the tree photo in Photoshop.
2. Use the Polygonal Lasso tool to trace the edge of the tree.
3. Use the Paint Bucket tool to fill in dark brown on the tree, as shown in Figure 7.12. Dark brown is used because the color tone of the hardwood floor is brown. Therefore, the shadows on the hardwood floor should be brown in tone. If the floor color tone is gray, then the shadows should be gray in tone.
4. Select the brown-colored tree, then use Edit > Copy and Edit > Paste to add it to your drawing. Use Edit > Transform > Distort to make the tree look like a shadow on the floor, as shown in Figure 7.13.
5. After adjusting the perspective for the brown tree to match the perspective of your drawing, rename the layer "shadow-tree." Change the **opacity** to 62% to make the shadow transparent so that the texture of the hardwood floor shows through (Figure 7.14).
6. Use the same procedure to add shadows for people. Make sure the shadows' color is brown and transparent. Rename each layer after you add shadows to people, such as "shadow-person-calling," as shown in Figure 7.15.

Figure 7.12

Figure 7.13

Figure 7.14

Figure 7.15

Figure 7.16

7. Use the Gradient Fill tool to add gray color to the column. Make the background layer, and use the Magic Wand tool to select the column. Then create a new layer called "column" and put gradient gray color on it to convey the impression that the column is rounded, as shown in Figure 7.16. Note that the lighting source is from the right side. Therefore, the left side of the column should be the darker area and the right side of the column should be lighter.

8. After adding all the entourages, add lighting effects to your drawing. See Chapter 5 for more detailed information about lighting.

Figure 7.17 is another example of adding entourage to a drawing. The figure is a refined version of Figure 7.8, which was produced in SketchUp (see Figure 7.18). Note that in Figure 7.17 the tree's color has been modified.

To change the color for the tree, go to Image > Adjustments > **Color Balance.** The dialogue box shown in Figure 7.19 appears. Move the sliders to change the values for different colors until the desired result is achieved. Note that a warm color tone is used for the tree in this drawing because the other color hues are warm.

Figure 7.20 shows yet another example of adding entourage and is a refined version of Figure 7.21, created in SketchUp. Note that the tree's color has been modified to a gray hue. Also note the shadow on a vertical wall.

Figure 7.17

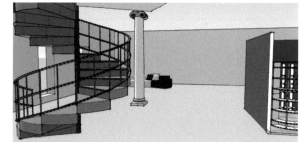

Figure 7.18

Figure 7.19

Figure 7.20

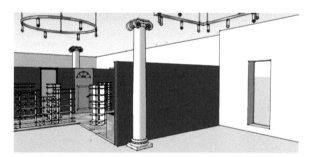

Figure 7.21

To change the tree to grayscale, select Image > Mode > **Grayscale.** The dialogue box shown in Figure 7.22 appears. Click Discard. The tree becomes grayscale, as shown in Figure 7.20.

Creating Shadows on a Vertical Wall

Creating a shadow on a vertical wall involves two steps. The first step is to create the shadow for the bottom part of the object on the floor; this involves the same procedure introduced in earlier examples. The second step is to create the shadow for the top part, or "rest part," of

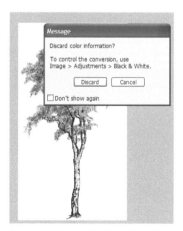

Figure 7.22

the object on the vertical wall. The "rest part" refers to the shadow projected on the vertical wall if the bottom of the object's shadow is projected on the floor. The following example shows how to create shadows on a vertical wall.

1. Use the Polygonal Lasso tool to trace the outline of the column, and use the Paint Bucket tool to fill in the gray color, as shown in Figure 7.23. Make sure the gray color is on a new layer.
2. Rename the new layer 1 "column-shadow-bottom." Duplicate this layer and rename it "column-shadow-top." Move one column to the side, as shown in Figure 7.24.

3. Use Edit > Transform > Distort to make the gray column look like a shadow on the floor. Refer to Chapter 5 on adding cast shadows for the detailed procedure. Change the opacity to 66%. Then use the Rectangular Marquee tool to select the portion of the column shadow on the wall, as shown in Figure 7.25.
4. Press Backspace to remove this portion of the shadow, as shown in Figure 7.26.
5. Use the Rectangular Marquee tool to select the lower portion of the column, as shown in Figure 7.27.
6. Press Backspace to remove the lower portion of the column. See Figure 7.28.

Figure 7.23

Figure 7.24

Figure 7.25

Figure 7.26

Figure 7.27

Figure 7.28

Figure 7.29

7. Then deselect and move the remaining shadow over to the wall so that it sits on top of the distorted bottom half. Change the opacity to 66%, as shown in Figure 7.29.

Adding Vehicles and Signage to a Drawing

Adding vehicles and signage to a drawing is another technique designers need to know. In Figure 7.30 cars, signage, and people have been added in Photoshop. The rough drawing shown in Figure 7.31 was created in SketchUp. The following shows how to add cars and signage.

1. Open the perspective drawing, shown in Figure 7.31, in Photoshop.
2. Use the Gradient Fill tool to add gray color to the ceiling area and the wall on the left side. Bring in exterior views that can be seen through the windows, as shown in Figure 7.32. See Chapter 3 for the detailed procedure of adding exterior views.

Figure 7.30

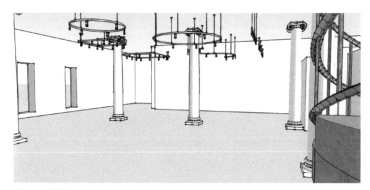

Figure 7.31

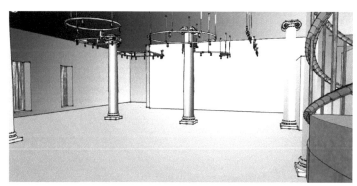

Figure 7.32

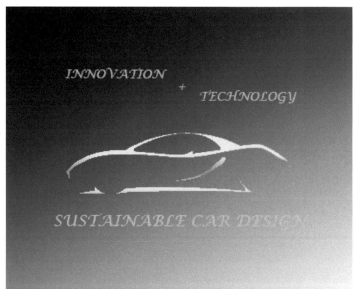

Figure 7.33

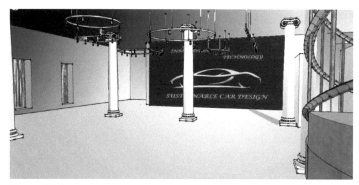

Figure 7.34

3. Create signage as shown in Figure 7.33.

4. Open the perspective drawing. Use the Magic Wand tool to select the back wall. Then select **Copy > Paste Special > Paste Into** to add the signage. Use Edit > Transform > Perspective to adjust the perspective. Your drawing should look like Figure 7.34.

5. Open the car photo in Photoshop. Click on the white background with the Magic Wand tool. Then right-click and choose Select Inverse. Only the yellow car will be selected. Select Edit > Copy, as shown in Figure 7.35.

6. Open the perspective drawing. Go to Edit > Paste to paste the yellow car into your drawing. Then use

Figure 7.35

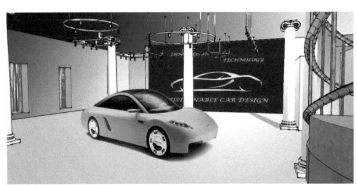

Figure 7.36

Figure 7.37

Figure 7.38

Edit > Transform > Scale to make the car larger or smaller, as shown in Figure 7.36.

7. Use the same procedure to add the black car to your perspective. See Figure 7.37.

8. Use the Gradient Fill tool to add gray gradient fill on the columns. Add people to the drawing, as shown in Figure 7.38.

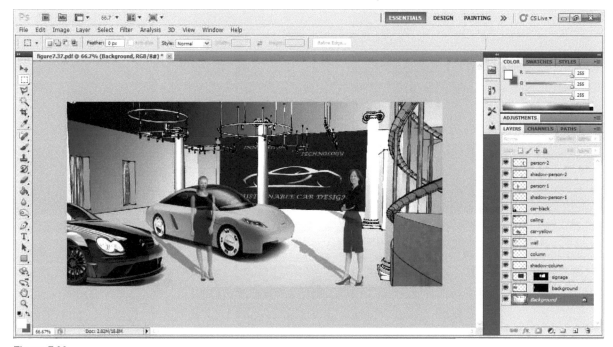

Figure 7.39

9. Add shadows to the people and the column, as shown in Figure 7.39. The procedure is the same as adding shadow to the chair on the floor in a previous chapter (refer to the section on creating cast shadows in Chapter 5 for detailed instructions). The Layers panel on the right side of the screen shows you all the layers and any effects applied.

Summary

This chapter demonstrated how to add entourage such as people, trees, and vehicles. The chapter also showed how to create shadows for entourages, especially on a vertical wall. The following summarizes the procedures covered:

- **Adding people.** Use Copy and Paste to bring in people. If there is a background behind the figures, use the Polygonal Lasso tool to trace the edge of the people. Then copy and paste them into to a new drawing.

- **Adding trees.** Use Copy and Paste to bring trees into your drawing.

- **Adding signage.** Use Copy and Paste Into to bring in signage. Use Edit > Transform > Perspective to adjust the perspective.

- **Adding vehicles.** Use Copy and Paste to bring in a car. Use Edit > Transform > Scale to adjust the size of the car.

- **Creating shadow on a vertical wall.** There are two steps in this process. Create the bottom portion of

the shadow on the floor first. Use the Paint Bucket tool to fill in the gray color in the object outline. Change the layer opacity to about 65%. Use Edit > Transform > Distort to adjust the perspective of the shadow on the floor. Then create the upper portion of the shadow on the wall. Use the Paint Bucket tool to fill in the gray color in the object outline. Change the layer opacity to 65%. Use the Move tool to move the upper portion shadow to the desired position.

Key Terms

Color Balance
Copy > Paste Special > Paste Into
Edit > Transform > Scale
Gradient Fill tool
Grayscale
Opacity
Polygonal Lasso tool

Projects

1. Use the drawing provided on the book's companion website http://www.bloomsbury.com/us/photoshop-for-interior-designers-9781609015442/ to add entourage to the perspective. The entourages include people and trees.

2. Create signage and add it to your perspective drawing. Also add vehicles.

3. Use the drawings in your studio project and add entourages to these drawings.

8

Working with Freehand Drawings

Chapter 8 introduces techniques for creating presentation drawings from freehand sketching, such as freehand-drawn elevations and sections as well as perspectives. Materials, background, and entourages will be added to the transformed digital drawings in Photoshop. Special effects such as watercolor will be applied to drawings as well. The edited drawings feature characteristics of both freehand drawings and digital drawings. The transformed drawings present the human touch and imperfections in the digital format. The following example of the Pantheon's exterior perspective is created by freehand sketching first and is then edited and enhanced in Photoshop (see Figure 8.1).

Transforming Freehand Drawings to Digital Drawings

Freehand sketching represents characteristics of human touch, personality through strokes and lines, and imperfections in the drawing. This is something that technology or computer software cannot replace. In order to represent the characteristics of freehand drawings in digital drawings, a new approach is necessary. The detailed procedure of transforming freehand drawings to digital drawings is as follows:

1. Create a freehand drawing for the Pantheon's exterior perspective, as shown in Figure 8.2.
2. Scan the freehand drawing into a PDF file for Photoshop use.
3. In Photoshop, use the Gradient tool to apply different colors in the drawing, as shown in Figure 8.3. If the boundary is not closed, use the Polygonal Lasso tool to draw outlines in order to create a closed boundary.
4. Flatten the image in Photoshop by selecting Layer > **Flatten Image.**

Figure 8.1

Figure 8.2

Figure 8.3

5. Use the Filter options to create special effects. The drawing in Figure 8.1 was created with the Smudge Stick artistic filter. Select Filter > Artistic > Smudge Stick. See Figure 8.4.

6. Click OK, as shown in Figure 8.4. Your drawing should look like the watercolor drawing in Figure 8.1.

Creating a Poster Using a Freehand Drawing—Building Section

Freehand drawings can be transformed into digital drawings and used in poster drawing. Figure 8.5 is an example that was created in Photoshop. The building section was initially drawn freehand. The following is the procedure for the drawing creation process.

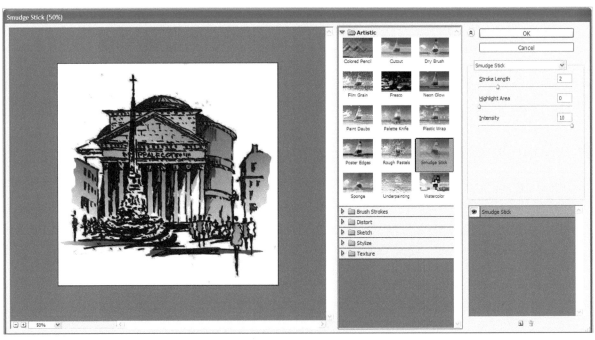

Figure 8.4

Figure 8.5

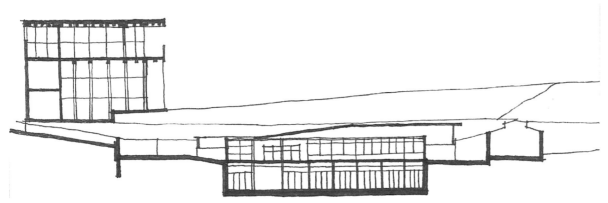

Figure 8.6

Creating a Digital Building Section from a Freehand Drawing

1. Create a freehand-drawn building section, as shown in Figure 8.6.
2. Scan the building section to a PDF file for Photoshop use.
3. Open Photoshop. Go to File > New. A dialogue box appears, as shown in Figure 8.7. You might want to set the resolution at 300 dpi for good-quality printing results. You also can set up your drawing size by adjusting the width and height values. Select **CMYK Color** in **Color Mode.** Click OK.
4. A new blank drawing appears. Go to **File > Place.** You can now browse the building section drawing. Select the building section drawing where you have already saved it. Note that the building section has been placed in the new blank drawing with a big X on top of it, as shown in Figure 8.8.
5. Press Enter. The X disappears.

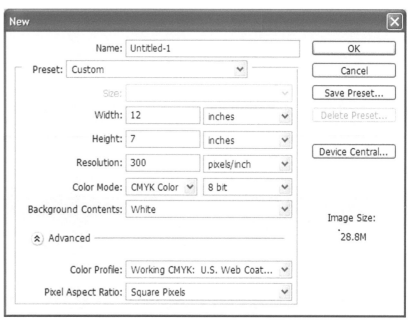

Figure 8.7

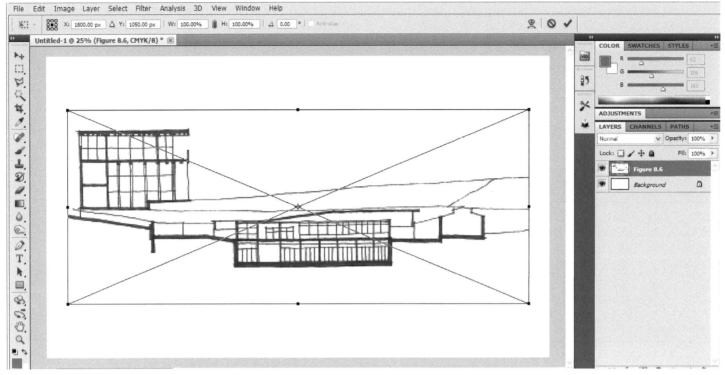

Figure 8.8

6. Use the Gradient Fill tool to fill in windows and walls on separate layers with different colors, as shown in Figure 8.9.

7. Apply stone wall material and ground material to the drawing. Make sure each material is on its own individual layer, as shown in Figure 8.10.

Figure 8.9

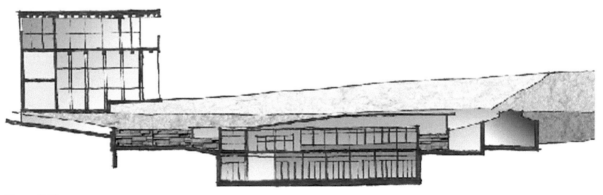

Figure 8.10

Figure 8.11

8. Add trees and people. Make sure each object is on a different layer. Pay attention to the size of the human figures. See Figure 8.11. Before you bring in the finished section to the poster, flatten the image.

Composing a Building Section in a Poster in Photoshop

The building section is an important component in presentation drawings. It represents the spatial relationship of the building, as well as the heights of each level, which cannot be presented on the floor plan. The following demonstrates a quick way to put a building section in a poster in Photoshop.

1. Open a new drawing in Photoshop. Set the resolution at 300 dpi and the appropriate page size as needed. Bring the background into Photoshop. You can use Copy and Paste as shown in Figure 8.12. (Note: The background in Figure 8.12 has been applied by watercolor effect.)

2. Create a new layer. Use the Rectangular Marquee tool to draw a rectangle in the white area. Then use the Gradient Fill tool to fill in the blue gradient fill as shown in Figure 8.13.

3. Use Copy and Paste to paste the building section into your poster drawing as in Figure 8.14. Use the Magic Wand tool and click on the building section background. Then right-click and select Layers >

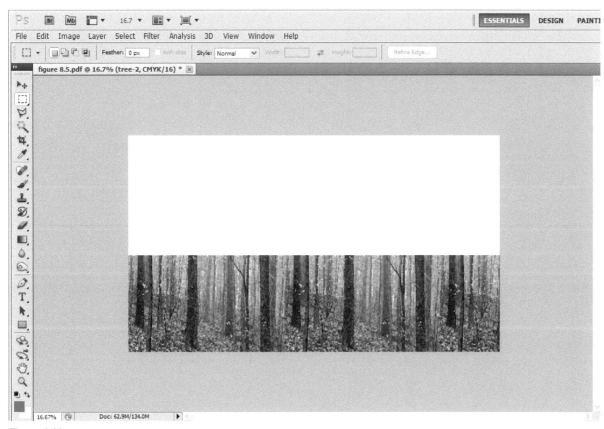

Figure 8.12

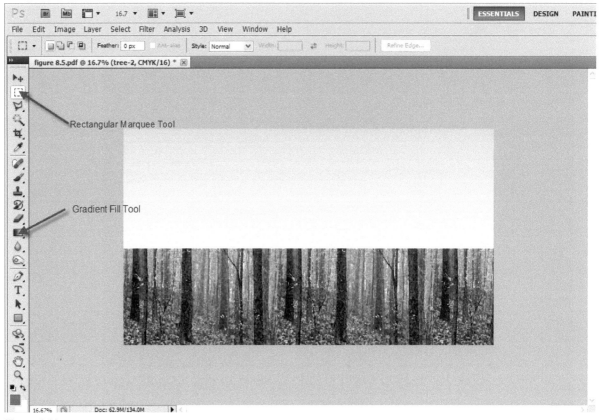

Figure 8.13

Figure 8.14

Figure 8.15

Multiply. Now the building section is selected without the white background. Paste the building section without the background into your poster.

4. Add trees and text in your poster drawing. Make sure each object is on a separate layer. You can add a couple of green trees to add more color. See Figure 8.15.

Creating a Poster Using a Freehand Drawing— Elevation and Perspective

Freehand-drawn elevations and perspectives also can be transformed into digital format in Photoshop. Figure 8.16 was created using freehand drawings of elevations and perspective. The elevations and perspective were drawn freehand first, then edited in Photoshop. The following is the process.

Creating a Digital Drawing from a Freehand Elevation

1. Create a freehand-drawn building elevation, as shown in Figure 8.17.
2. Scan the elevation as a PDF file for Photoshop use.
3. Open Photoshop. Go to File > New. A dialogue box appears, as shown in Figure 8.7. Set the resolution at 300 dpi if you want good-quality printing results. You also can set your drawing size by adjusting width and height values. For Color Mode, select CMYK Color. Click OK.

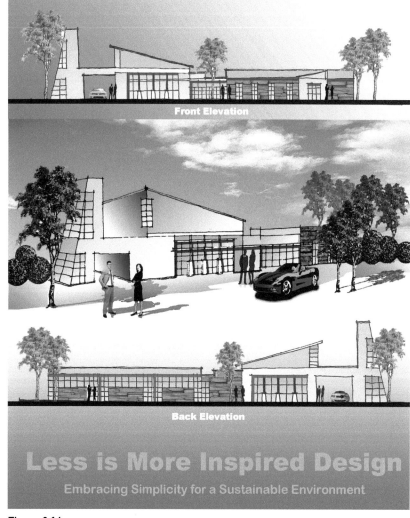

Figure 8.16

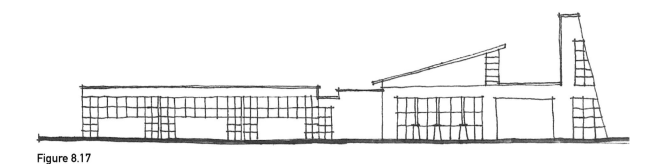

Figure 8.17

Figure 8.18

4. A new blank drawing appears. Go to File > Place to browse the building elevation drawing. Select the building elevation drawing. Note that the elevation has been placed in the new blank drawing with a big X on it, as shown in Figure 8.18.

5. Press Enter. The X disappears.

6. Go to Layers, click on the small drop-down menu, and select Multiply, as shown in Figure 8.19. Then click on the small Lock icon and lock the layer.

7. Use the Gradient Fill tool to fill in windows and walls on separate layers with different colors, as shown in Figure 8.20.

8. Apply stone wall material to the drawing. Make sure that each material is on an individual layer. See Figure 8.21.

9. Add trees and human figures as well as the car in the drawing. Make sure each object is on a different layer. Pay attention to the size of human figures. See Figure 8.22. Before bringing the finished elevation into the poster, flatten the image.

Figure 8.19

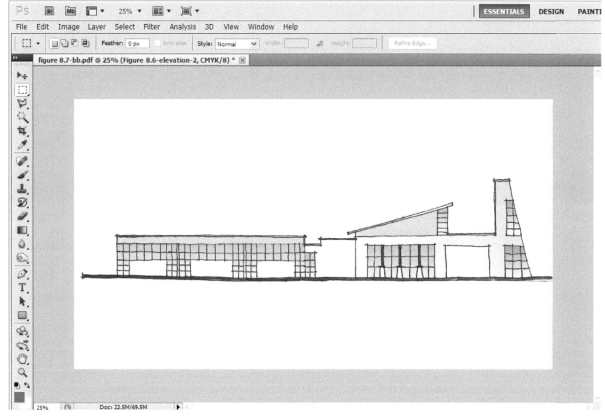

Figure 8.20

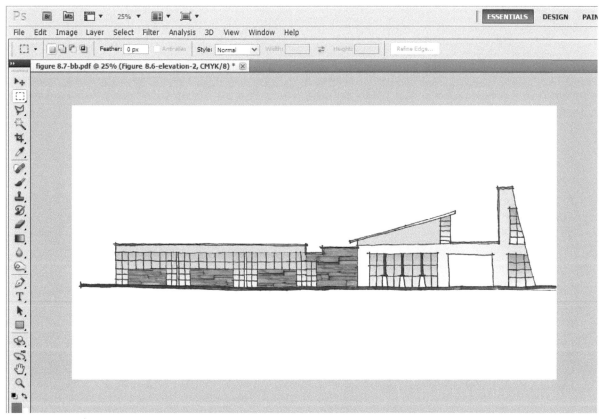

Figure 8.21

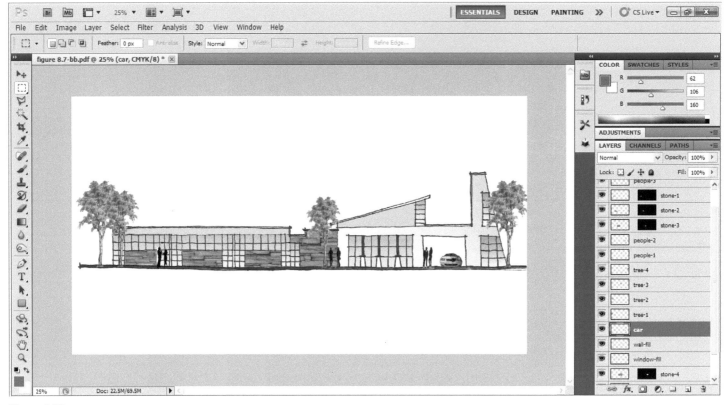

Figure 8.22

Figure 8.23

Figure 8.24

10. The last step is to add shadows to the elevation. You can create a new layer called "shadow" and make the opacity 70% so that the shadow is transparent. Use the Paint Bucket tool to fill in the gray color. The finished elevation should look like Figure 8.23.

11. Follow the same procedure to create the other elevation. The finished elevation should look like Figure 8.24.

Creating a Digital Drawing from a Freehand Perspective

Building perspective is another important component in presentation drawings. It represents building materials and height, as well as spatial relationship. The following demonstrates a simple and quick way to create perspective drawings in Photoshop.

1. Create a freehand-drawn building elevation as shown in Figure 8.25.

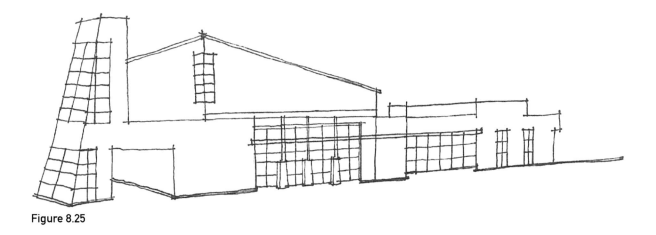

Figure 8.25

Figure 8.26

2. Scan the elevation to a PDF file for Photoshop use.

3. Open Photoshop. Go to File > New. A dialogue box appears, as shown in Figure 8.7. If you want good-quality printing results, set the resolution at 300 dpi. You also can set your drawing size by adjusting width and height values. For Color Mode, select CMYK Color. Click OK.

4. A new blank drawing appears. Go to File > Place. Now you can browse the building elevation drawing. Select the building elevation drawing. Note that the elevation has been placed in the new blank drawing with a big X on it, as shown in Figure 8.26.

5. Press Enter. The X disappears.

6. Go to Layers, click on the small drop-down menu, and select Multiply, as shown in Figure 8.19. Then click the small Lock icon and lock the layer.

7. Use the Gradient Fill tool to fill in windows and walls on separate layers with different colors. Also apply stone wall material to the drawing, as shown in Figure 8.27.

8. Add trees and bushes to the drawing. Make sure each object is on a different layer, as shown in Figure 8.28. You might want different colors and sizes of trees in order to portray the sense of distance in perspective drawing.

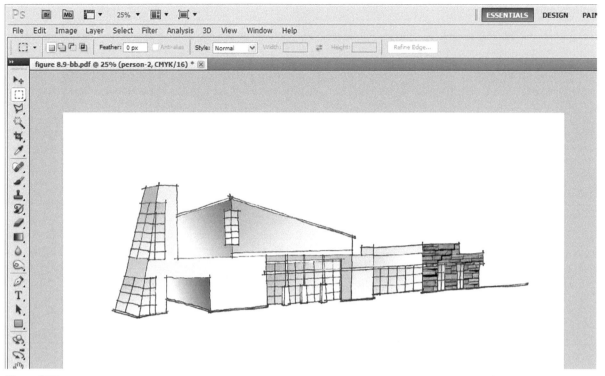

Figure 8.27

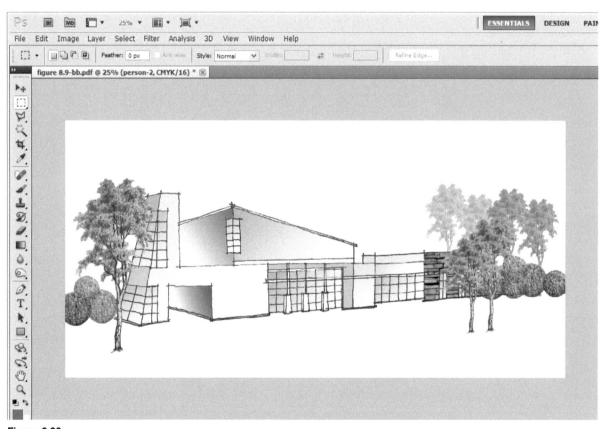

Figure 8.28

9. Add human figures and the car to your perspective drawing, as shown in Figure 8.29. Create separate layers for each object. Adjust the opacity to about 70% for each layer that contains entourage.

10. Add shadows for trees and human figures as well as shadows on the building. You also need to add the shadows on the ground. To do so, use the Polygon Lasso tool to draw the outline of the shadow and then use the Gradient Fill tool to fill in gray color. See Figure 8.30. Create separate layers for each object.

11. Add blue sky to your perspective in Photoshop. Use the Copy and Paste commands to bring in the blue sky, as shown in Figure 8.31. A blue sky image can

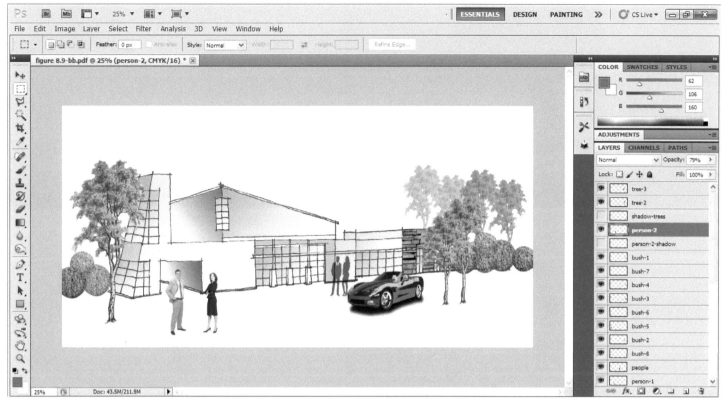

Figure 8.29

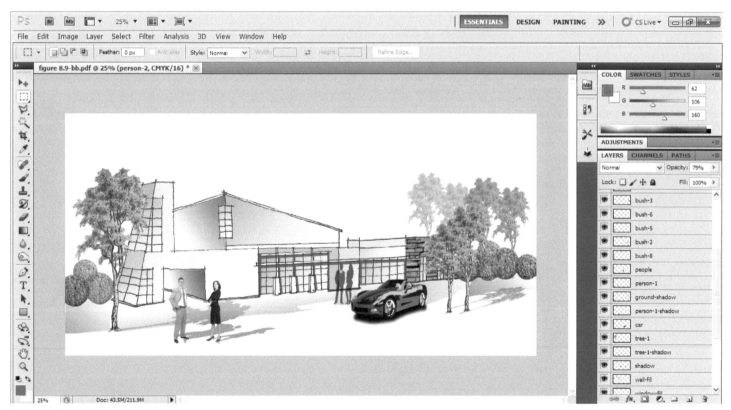

Figure 8.30

be downloaded from a website, such as in a Google image search.

12. Use the Filter options in Photoshop to create special effects, such as watercolor and pastel. Before doing so, however, you must flatten the image by going to Layer > Flatten Image. All the layers are combined into one single layer.

13. You also must make sure the Mode is set to RGB and **8 Bits/Channel** before applying artistic filters. To do so, select Image > Mode, as shown in Figure 8.32.

14. Now select Filter > Filter Gallery. When the dialogue box appears, select Watercolor. Your perspective should look like Figure 8.33.

Figure 8.31

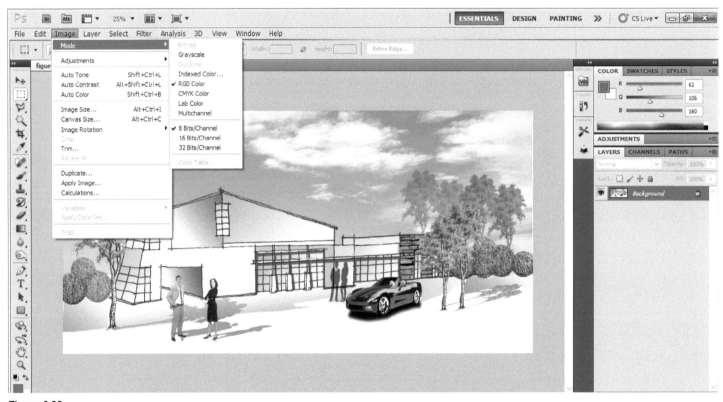

Figure 8.32

Composing Transformed Freehand Drawings in Photoshop

A good poster presentation drawing should contain floor plan, elevations, section, and perspective, or any combination of these. Depending on the project, sometimes building elevations and perspectives are combined as a poster presentation, as in the example that follows. Other times the floor plan and perspectives are combined. To combine elevations and perspective into one presentation in Photoshop, follow these steps:

1. Open a new drawing in Photoshop. Set the resolution at 300 and the appropriate page size as needed. Use the Copy command and, one at a time, copy the two transformed elevations and the transformed perspective into Photoshop, making sure to only select the images and not the backgrounds. To do so, click the background with the Magic Wand tool; then right-click and choose Select Inverse. Now only the elevation or perspective is selected and not the background.

Figure 8.33

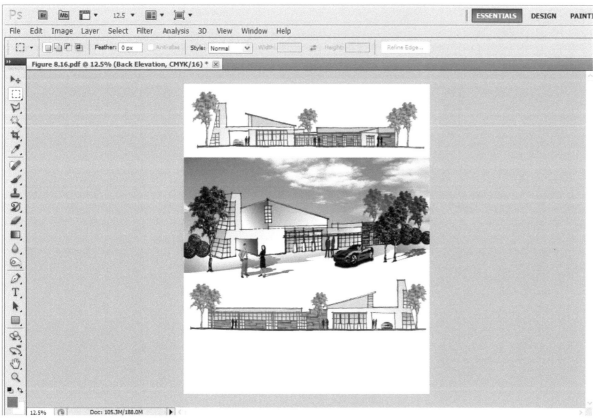

Figure 8.34

Paste the elevations and perspective into your poster as shown in Figure 8.34. Make sure each drawing is on a separate layer, and name them "elevation-1," "elevation-2," and "perspective."

2. Create a new layer called "background." Use the Rectangular Marquee tool to draw a rectangle in the white area. Then use the Gradient Fill tool to fill in blue gradient fill, as shown in Figure 8.35. Move

the "elevation-1" layer, the "elevation-2" layer, and the "perspective" layer on top of the "background" layer (they will appear above the "background" layer in the Layers palette list).

3. Using the Rectangle tool with a Stroke of black, draw a thick black line underneath each elevation. Then add text to your poster. As always, make sure each object is on a separate layer. See Figure 8.36.

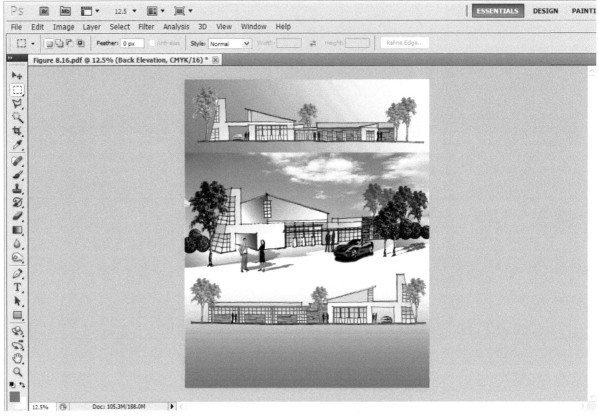

Figure 8.35

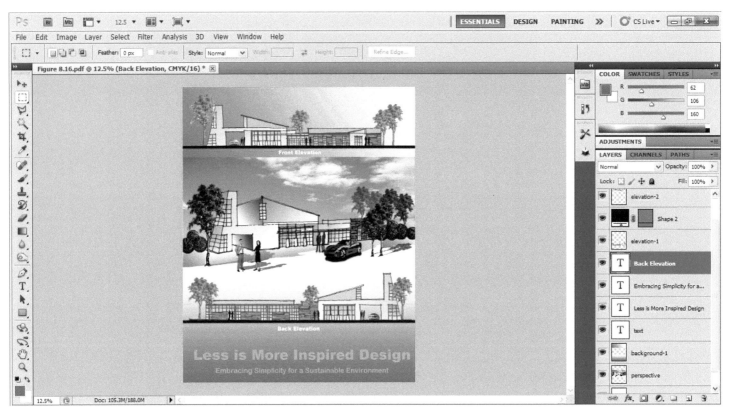

Figure 8.36

Summary

This chapter introduced techniques of transforming free-hand drawings to digital drawings in Photoshop. The addition of real materials and entourage to digital drawings was also discussed and demonstrated. Special effects such as watercolor can also be applied to the drawing, using the filters. The following subjects were discussed:

- Preparing freehand drawings
- Adding materials to drawings
- Adding entourage to drawings
- Adding special effects to drawings
- Composing a poster drawing in Photoshop

Key Terms

8 Bits/Channel
CMYK Color
Color Mode
Filter Gallery
File > Place
Flatten Image
Select Inverse

Projects

1. Compose a visual narrative poster that illustrates your design concept for a project you are working on. You may use a combination of both freehand drawings and digital drawings. In the poster, include the floor plan, the elevation, the section, and the perspective.

2. Use freehand-drawn floor plans, elevations, or perspectives that have been edited in Photoshop. Add materials and entourage to the transformed digital drawings.

3. Use Photoshop to compose a poster drawing that includes background, text, and all necessary drawings as described above.

9

Composing Drawings with InDesign

Chapter 9 introduces techniques for composing Photoshop drawings. Beginning with creating background, then composing the drawings with floor plans, elevations, isometric drawings, and perspectives or other relevant images, this chapter describes the procedure via step-by-step demonstrations. The focus of this chapter is on InDesign, which allows you to compose drawings you have created in Photoshop. As mentioned, InDesign is a software package specifically for page layout and composing drawings. You can also easily add text and graphic background to your presentation drawings with this program. For example, all the figures in Chapter 1 were created with InDesign. Because it is a flexible and powerful way to manipulate graphics and text, it is ideal for creating visual narratives that tell a story about your design.

InDesign Basics

In previous chapters, you learned how to create and refine individual drawings in Photoshop. Now you need to put all the individual drawings together in a poster format that will tell the story about your design. Because you only want to compose a poster, you do not have to know every single toolbar and procedure in InDesign, only how to:

- Set up a new drawing.

- Create a new **layer** for each object.

- Create background.

- Create a solid or gradient background.

- Import individual drawings.

- Add text.

Following are some fundamentals of InDesign you need to know before we delve into the demonstrations.

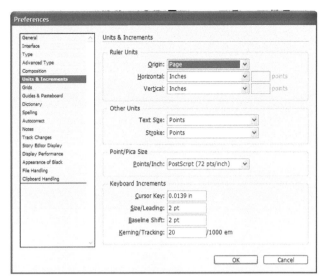

Figure 9.1

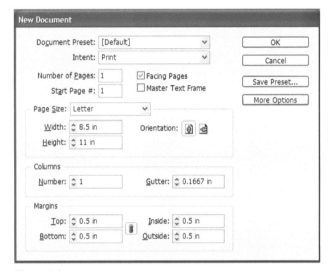

Figure 9.2

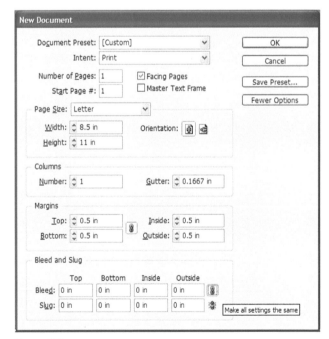

Figure 9.3

Creating a New Drawing

You can create a new poster presentation entirely in Photoshop. However, InDesign is specifically for page layout and provides more flexibility for more complex presentaions. The following shows how to create a new drawing in InDesign.

Before you set up a new page in InDesign, make sure that you are working with "inches" as units. Go to Edit > Preferences > Units & Increments. A dialog box appears, as shown Figure 9.1. In the Horizontal and Vertical drop-downs, select Inches. In the Origin drop-down, select Page.

1. Choose File > New > New Document. A New Document dialogue box appears, as shown in Figure 9.2. Settings include Document Preset, Margins, and Columns, as well as Bleed and Slug. These settings can be changed at any time.

The new document dialogue box consists of the Document Preset, Margins, and Columns as well as Bleed and Slug drop-downs, so that you can set up the page size, margins, and page columns all in one place. These settings can be changed at any time.

Specify Drawing Setup

To specify the dimensions of the **bleed** and **slug** areas, click More Options (if More Options is already selected, these areas will already be shown in the dialogue box). The bleed and slug areas extend out from the edges of the defined Page Size. To make the bleed or slug areas extend evenly on all sides, click the icon with the Make All Settings The Same tool tip, as shown in Figure 9.3. They will now appear with a chain icon. Following is an overview of the settings in the New Document dialogue box.

- ***Document Preset.*** This option allows you to choose a preset you have saved earlier. When you open a new document, the preset displays as default.

- ***Intent.*** The Print option is normally selected here. However, choosing the Web option changes several options in the dialogue box, such as turning off **Facing Pages**, changing the **orientation** from portrait to landscape, and using a page size based on monitor resolution (e.g., the units will now be in pixels, rather than inches). You can edit any of these settings, but you cannot change the **Intent** setting after the document is created.

- ***Number of Pages.*** Here you can specify the number of pages to create in the new document, as well as the page number on which the document starts. If you specify an even number (such as 2) with Facing Pages selected, the first spread in the document begins with a two-page spread.

- *Facing Pages.* Select this option to make left and right pages face each other in a double-page *spread*, such as for books and magazines. Deselect this option to let each page stand alone, such as when you're printing flyers or posters or when you want objects to bleed into the binding.

- *Page Size.* Choose a page size from the menu, or type values for Width and Height. Page size represents the final size you want after bleeds or other marks outside the page are trimmed.

- *Orientation.* Click Portrait (tall) or Landscape (wide). When Height is the larger value, the portrait icon is selected. When Width is the larger value, the landscape icon is selected. Clicking the deselected icon switches the Height and Width values.

- *Bleed.* The bleed area allows you to print objects that are placed at the outer edge of the defined page size. For a page of the required dimensions, if an object is positioned at its edge, some white may appear at the edge of the printed area because of slight misalignment during printing or trimming. You should therefore position the object a little beyond the edge, and trim after printing. The bleed area is shown by a red line on the document. You can specify this in the Bleed area of the Print dialogue box.

- *Slug.* The slug area is discarded when the document is trimmed to its final page size. This area contains printing information, customized color bar information, or other instructions and descriptions for other information in the document. Objects (including text frames) positioned in the slug area are printed but will disappear when the document is trimmed to its final page size. Objects outside the bleed or slug area (whichever extends farther) do not print.

Note: You can also click the Save Preset button to save document settings for future use. A dialogue box will appear that allows you to specify the name of the preset. See Figure 9.4.

2. Click OK to open a new document with the settings you specified. Figure 9.5 shows a new document with specified settings; it also uses a preset setting.

Define Document Presets

You can save drawing settings for page size, columns, margins, and bleed and slug areas in a preset to both save time and ensure consistency when creating similar drawings.

1. Choose File > **Document Presets** > Define. A dialogue box appears, as shown in Figure 9.6.
2. Click New.
3. Name the preset "Document Preset 2," and select basic layout options in the New Document Preset dialogue box, as shown in Figure 9.7.
4. Click OK in this box and the preceding Document Presets dialogue box.

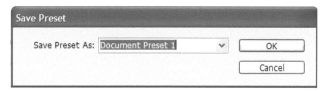

Figure 9.4

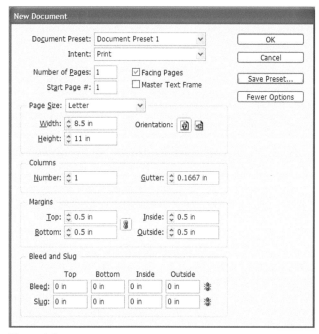

Figure 9.5

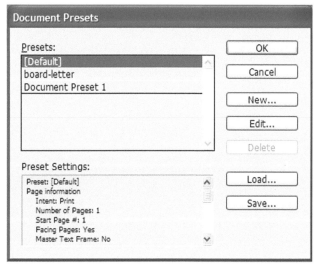

Figure 9.6

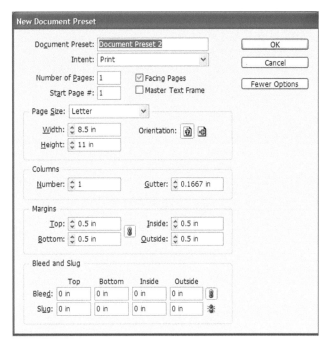

Figure 9.7

Creating New Layers

Each document includes at least one named **layer**. By using multiple layers, you can create and edit specific areas or types of content in your document without affecting other areas or content types. For example, if you need to make a minor change in a small area, you can isolate that layer and make the changes, or replace the individual image entirely. You can also use layers to display alternate design ideas for the same layout. Think of layers as transparent sheets stacked on top of each other. If a layer doesn't have objects on it, you can see "through" it to any objects on layers below it.

You can add layers at any time by highlighting any current layer, right-clicking, and selecting New Layer. Another option is to go to the Layers panel menu, as shown in Figure 9.8. Or you can use the Create New Layer button at the bottom of the Layers panel as shown in Figure 9.8. The number of layers a document can have is limited only by the RAM available to InDesign.

Now open the Layers panel:

1. Choose Window > Layers, as shown in Figure 9.9.
2. To create a new layer above the selected layer, click the Create New Layer icon as shown in Figure 9.9. You can drag the layer in the Layers panel above or below an existing layer.

Preparing the Background

Figure 1.1 in Chapter 1 was completed in InDesign after each individual drawing was created. The background fills with black color. To prepare the background:

1. Open a new drawing in InDesign. Set the Slug to 0 and the Bleed to 0.
2. Click the Rectangle tool on the left side of the tool bar, and drag to draw a box from the upper left corner to lower right corner of the slug area, as shown in Figure 9.10.

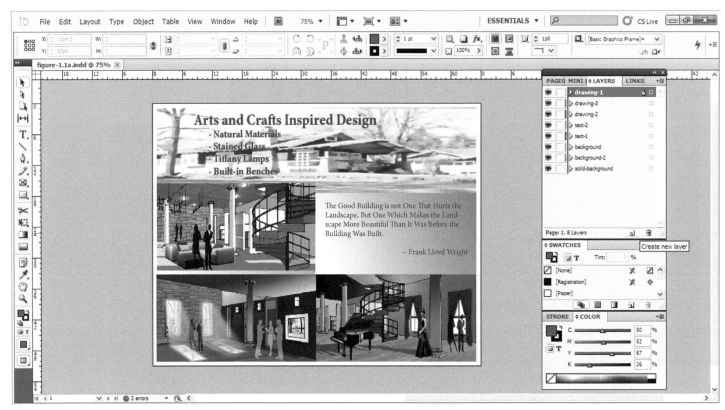

Figure 9.8

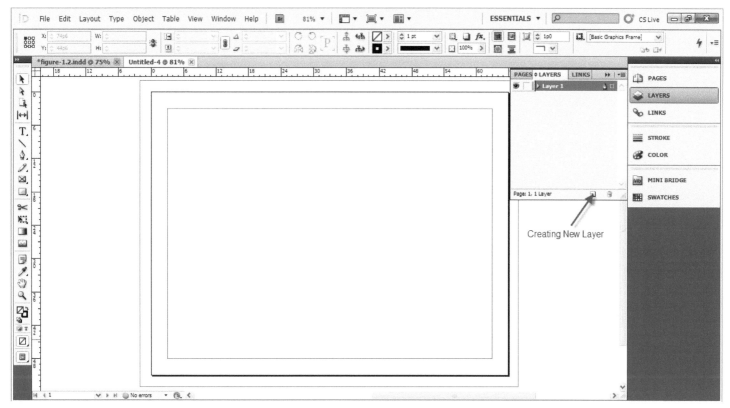

Figure 9.9

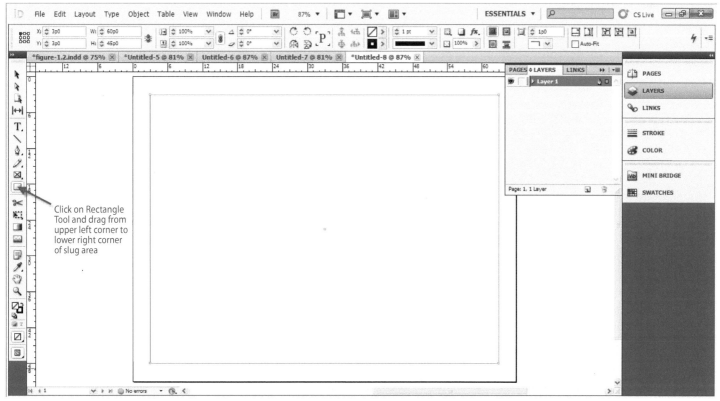

Figure 9.10

3. Double-click the small square on the left side of your screen to select the background color. A dialogue box appears, as shown in Figure 9.11. Click OK for a black background.

4. Double-click on the layer to rename it. A dialogue box appears, as shown in Figure 9.12. Type "background" in the Name field.

5. For practice, click on the small square on the layer named "background" to lock the layer. A Lock icon appears now next to the Eye sign in the Layers panel.

6. Next, making sure the layer named "background" is active, click on the Eye icon and Lock icon to turn off the layer and unlock the layer.

7. Create a new layer called "band-2."

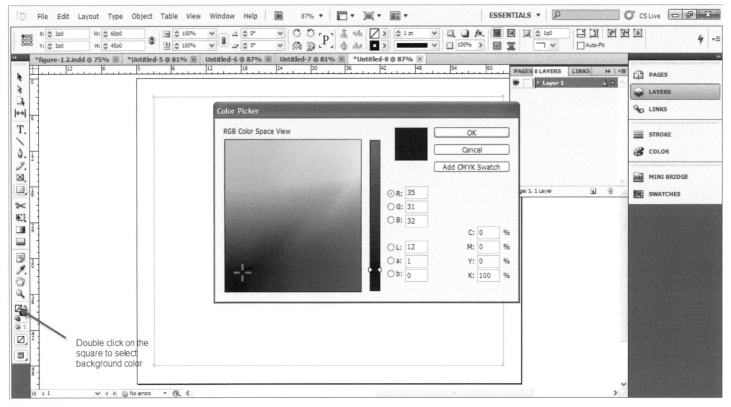

Double click on the square to select background color

Figure 9.11

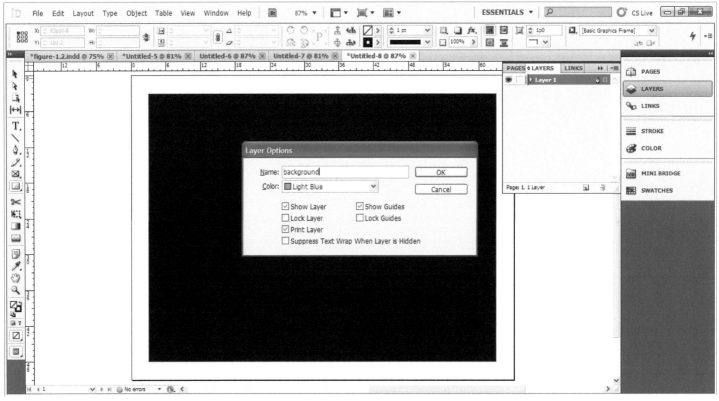

Figure 9.12

8. Select the **Rectangle Frame tool** on the left-side tool bar, and drag it to create a rectangle frame in a blue line, as shown in Figure 9.13. Now select the **Gradient Swatch tool** to add a gradient fill to the blue-line rectangle, as shown in Figure 9.13.

Note: When you use the Rectangle Frame tool to draw the frame, usually the frames are visible. If you want to turn the frames off, right-click on the last square on the tool bar on the left side of your screen and select Preview, as shown in Figure 9.14. This hides all the frames.

Figure 9.13

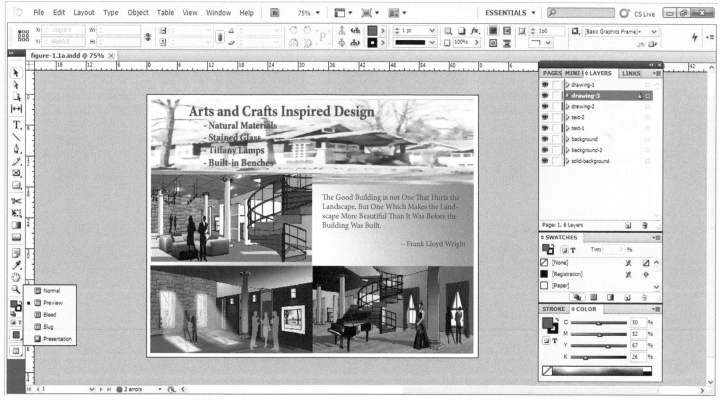

Figure 9.14

9. Use the same procedure to create another gradient background on layer "band-1," as shown in Figure 9.15. Click on the Eye and Lock icons to show the "background" layer and lock it, shown in Figure 9.16.

Adding Individual Images to Layers

Any new object or new individual image has to be placed on the **target layer**, which appears in the Layers panel, with a Pen icon. You can add individual images to the target layer by any of the following methods:

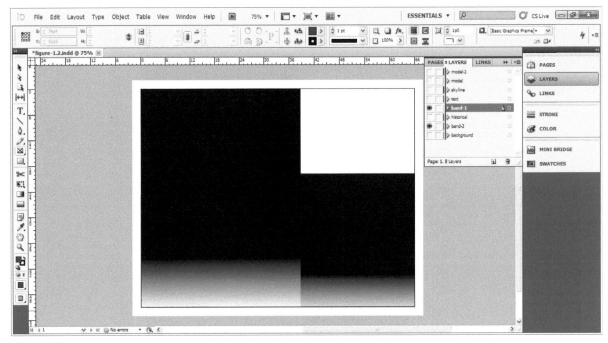

Figure 9.15

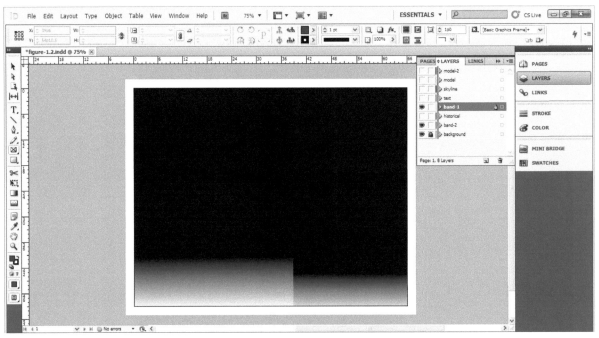

Figure 9.16

- Creating new objects with the Type tool or drawing tools

- Importing, placing, or pasting text or graphics

- Selecting objects on other layers and then moving them to the new layer

You cannot draw or place a new object on a hidden or locked layer. When you select a drawing tool or the Type tool, or place a file when the target layer is hidden or locked, the pointer changes to the crossed-out-pencil icon when it is positioned over the document window. Either show or unlock the target layer, or target a visible, unlocked layer. If you choose Edit > Paste when the target layer is hidden or locked, an alert message gives you the choice of showing or unlocking the target layer. When you click a layer in the Layers panel to target it, the Pen icon appears on the layer you clicked, and the layer also highlights to indicate that it is targeted.

Creating Presentation Drawings Using Multiple Software Programs

Chapter 10 introduces techniques for creating presentation drawings using 3D modeling programs along with Photoshop. In this chapter, using Trimble SketchUp to create a rough 3D model is demonstrated, followed by using Photoshop to refine and modify the perspective drawing. The chapter also discusses how to use InDesign to compose a poster that presents the design concept and tells the story of an entire design process. In many cases, the drawings are created and refined in several different combinations of programs. Specifically:

- Using AutoCAD drawings in Trimble SketchUp

- Using Trimble SketchUp drawings in Photoshop

- Using AutoCAD drawings in Photoshop

- Composing posters in InDesign

SketchUp Fundamentals

Before delving into the demonstration, you must know the basic command buttons in **SketchUp**. When you launch SketchUp, a dialogue box appears asking you to choose a template. Select the Architectural Design—Feet and Inches template.

Figure 10.1 shows the command buttons and their locations. Their functions are explained in the following demonstration.

As mentioned, Trimble SketchUp is a free software program, and most 3D models in this book were created in SketchUp first and then refined in Photoshop. AutoCAD's native file format is DWG, and you will need the Trimble SketchUp Pro version to import DWG floor plans from AutoCAD. The very preliminary floor plan drawing in Figure 10.1 was imported from AutoCAD for this demonstration. You may not need to do anything special when importing the DWG floor plan drawing, but a small amount of preparation often helps make the import process more efficient.

SketchUp automatically discards any entities in the imported CAD file that has no 3D relevance, such as text, dimensioning, hatching, and logos. However, SketchUp does not discard the layers holding these entities, so you may want to delete those layers from the CAD file prior to **import**, or you can easily delete them all in SketchUp after importing by opening the Layers browser (Window > Layers) and using the Purge command on the menu, which purges all unused layers.

Importing 2D DWG Files to SketchUp

Importing a 2D drawing from **AutoCAD** into SketchUp simplifies the drawing creation process. You can build three-dimensional walls based on the floor plan imported in SketchUp.

To import a 2D DWG floor plan file from AutoCAD:

1. Select File > Import. The Open dialogue box appears.
2. If desired, click the Options button to modify the import options, such as units, for the incoming file.
3. Click OK to import the file. The Import Results dialogue box appears, containing details of the imported model or drawing.

Note: It can take several minutes to import a large file because SketchUp's native geometry is very different from most CAD software and the conversion process is calculation-intensive.

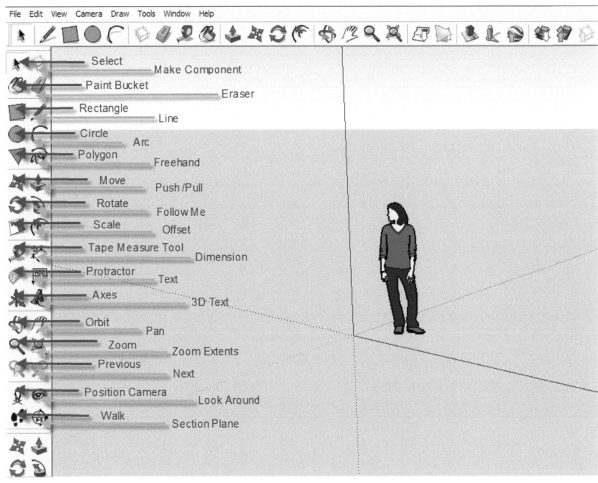

Figure 10.1

4. Click OK. The model or floor plan appears in the drawing area at the origin.
5. Click the **Zoom Extents** tool to locate the imported model if it is not currently displayed in your drawing area.

You also can import AutoCAD drawings in TIFF and JPG format to older versions of SketchUp. Simply go to File > Import on top of the toolbar. In the dialogue box that opens, browse for the AutoCAD file and select the file format type, such as TIFF or JPG. TIFF format generally is recommended because it is better quality. TIFF is a better choice for archiving images when all details must be preserved.

Figure 10.2 is a floor plan created first in AutoCAD and then imported from AutoCAD to SketchUp. The two sofas are imported from the SketchUp 3D model library.

Using AutoCAD Drawings in SketchUp

As mentioned, the floor plan in Figure 10.2 was created in AutoCAD first and then imported to SketchUp. After importing the floor plan, you can create three-dimensional walls and other objects. You also can view the perspective from different angles. In addition, SketchUp provides a library of premade 3D furniture or other objects. The following demonstrates how to build a 3D model in SketchUp and insert premade models.

Isometric View

After importing a 2D floor plan, you can build 3D walls in **isometric view**, as shown in Figure 10.3. To see your floor plan in an isometric view, click the **Orbit** button as shown in the figure.

Creating 3D Walls

In an isometric view, it is very easy to create a 3D wall. Click the **Rectangle** button on the toolbar on the left of your screen, as shown in Figure 10.3. Trace the wall section on the floor plan to draw a rectangle. It is now filled with a gray solid color. Now click the **Push/Pull** button as shown in the figure. Place the stamplike tool (a cube with red arrow) on top of the solid gray area just drawn. Note that small black dots appear on the gray area to show it is selected. Drag the black-dotted area to form a wall, as shown in Figure 10.4.

Inserting Premade 3D Models

After you have created all the walls, you also can insert some premade 3D models into your drawing, such as furniture, columns, and other architectural components. Figure 10.5 shows premade 3D models, such as sofas and columns, that have been inserted into SketchUp.

To insert the models, select File > **3D Warehouse** > Get Models. A dialogue box appears. Type in a key word, such as "sofa" or "column," and click Search. A dialogue

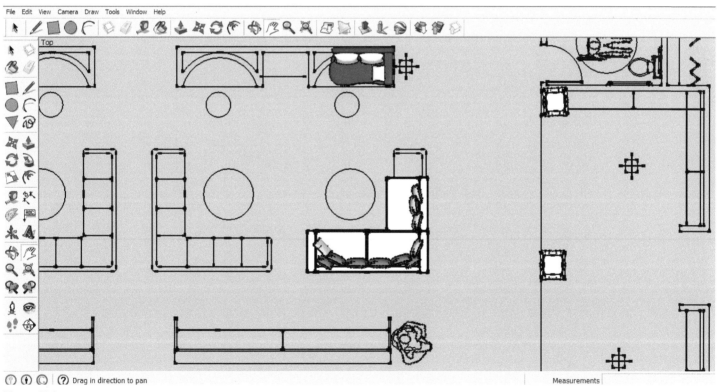

Figure 10.2

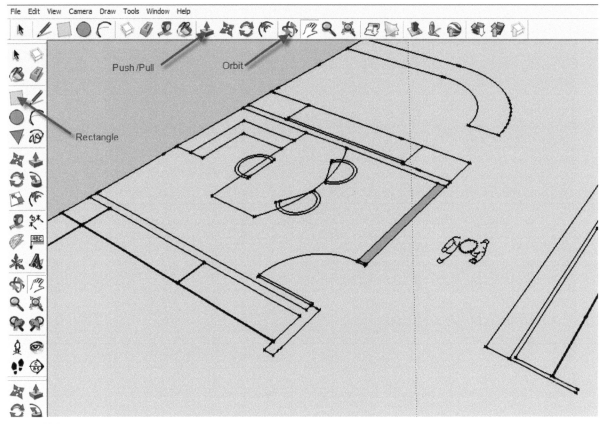

Figure 10.3

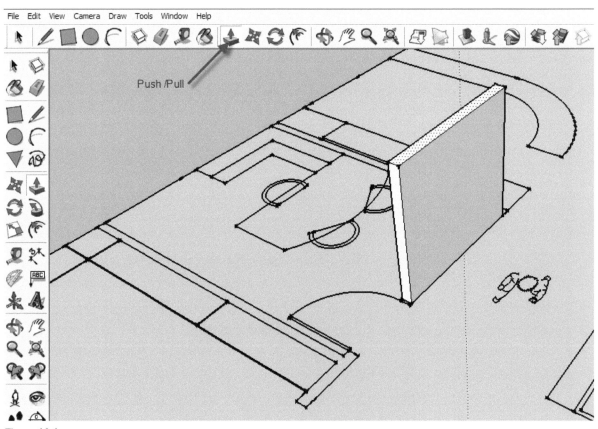

Figure 10.4

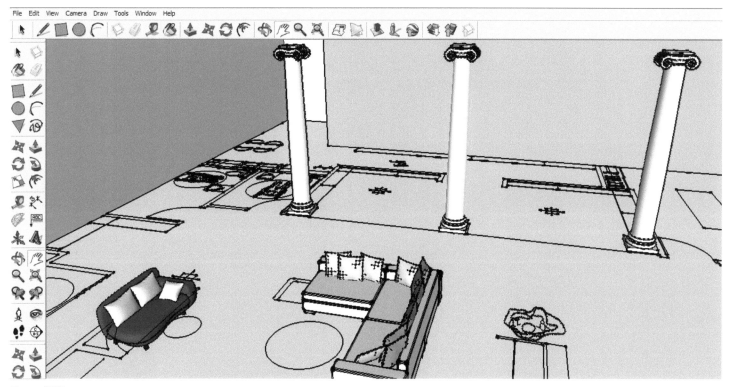

File Edit View Camera Draw Tools Window Help

Figure 10.5

box appears, as shown in Figure 10.6. Click Download Model next to the object you want to bring into your drawing. After downloading the object in SketchUp, you also can scale the object to the desired size.

Creating Windows or Doors in SketchUp

Sometimes you will need to create window or doors in SketchUp. The process is very simple and straightforward:

- Use the Rectangle tool to draw a rectangle on the wall, as shown in Figure 10.7.

- Click the Push/Pull button and place your cursor on top of the rectangle you just created. The rectangle area is now highlighted with small blue dots, as shown in Figure 10.8.

- Push your cursor toward the outside of the building. You will see a rectangular hole on the wall, as shown in Figure 10.9.

Creating Perspective Views in SketchUp

After creating the walls and ceiling and inserting premade 3D objects, you can easily create **perspective views** in SketchUp. Click the **Position Camera** button to create a perspective view. Then use **Zoom** to adjust the distance from the camera to the object, as shown in Figure 10.10.

To scale an object, click the **Scale** button, as shown in Figure 10.10. The Scale feature allows you to change the size of the object. After creating the perspective, you can also click the **Look Around** button to create a different perspective, as shown in Figure 10.11.

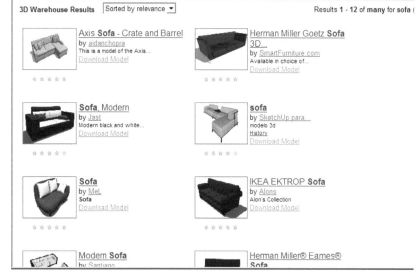

Figure 10.6

Adding Materials to Drawings in SketchUp

You also can add **materials** from the materials library (although you can also add materials later in Photoshop). Figure 10.12 is an example of brick wall material that has been applied in SketchUp.

To add materials on the wall or floor, select Window > Materials from the toolbar at the top of your screen. A Materials dialogue box appears, as shown in Figure 10.13. Select a category, such as brick and cladding, from the drop-down menu. Several choices of materials will be listed. Click the material you want to apply to the wall

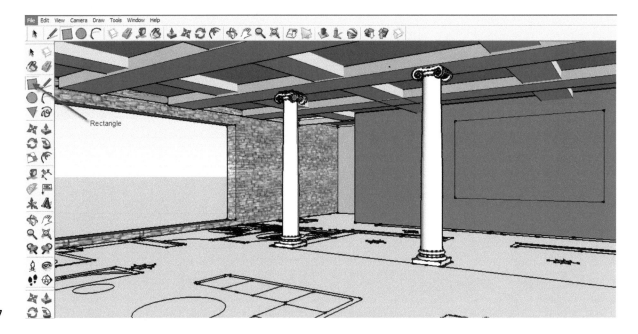

Figure 10.7

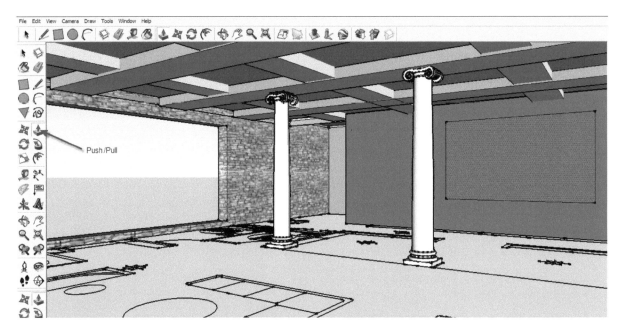

Figure 10.8

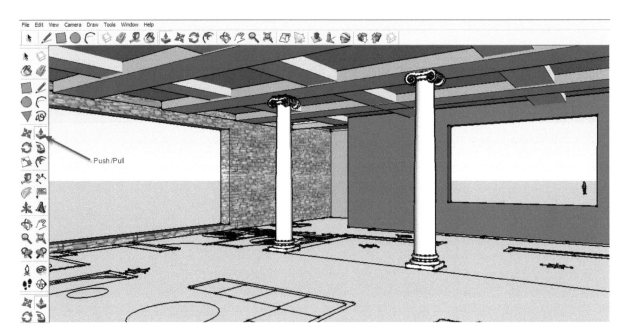

Figure 10.9

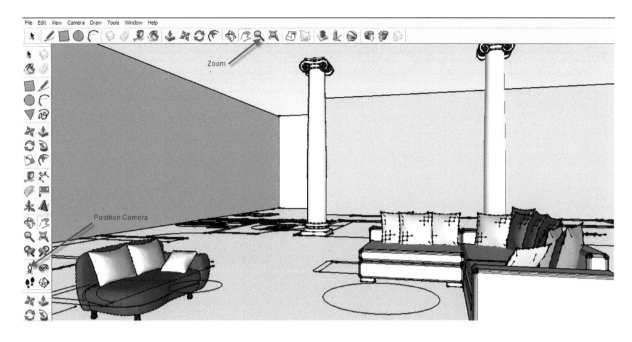

Figure 10.10

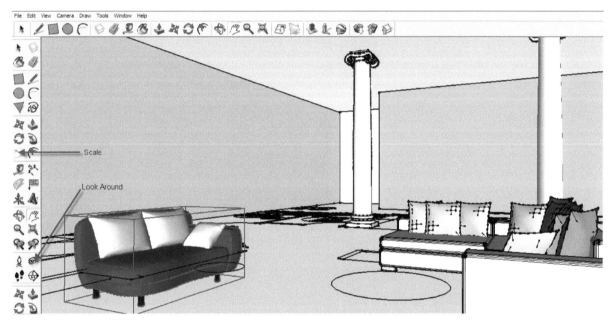

Figure 10.11

Figure 10.12

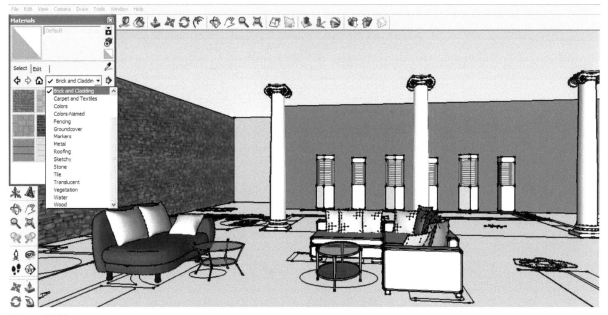

Figure 10.13

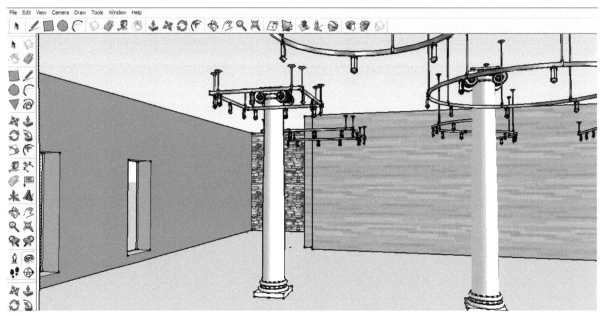

Figure 10.14

or floor. You will now have a **Paint Bucket** icon on your cursor. Place your cursor on top of the surface where you want to apply the material, and click on the surface. That material is then applied to that surface.

You can also apply different colors to the wall or floor in SketchUp. Figure 10.14 shows applied color (green) and applied materials (brick and wood panel) on the walls.

Creating Shadows in SketchUp

SketchUp also allows you to add shadows to your perspective drawing. Shadows create a strong sense of contrast and a dramatic lighting effect. Figures 10.15 and 10.16 are two examples of shadows that have been added in perspective.

To add shadows to your perspective drawing, select View > **Shadows**. The shadow effects are added to your perspective drawing, as shown in Figure 10.17.

Bringing SketchUp to Photoshop

After finishing a rough perspective in SketchUp, you can export the perspective drawing to **TIFF** format; this will allow you to enhance it with materials and lightings in Photoshop. To export a drawing from SketchUp, select File > Export > **2D Graphic**, as shown in Figure 10.18.

A dialogue box appears, asking for the 2D file destination. Specify the file destination and click **Export**. A 2D TIFF file is saved in the location you specified.

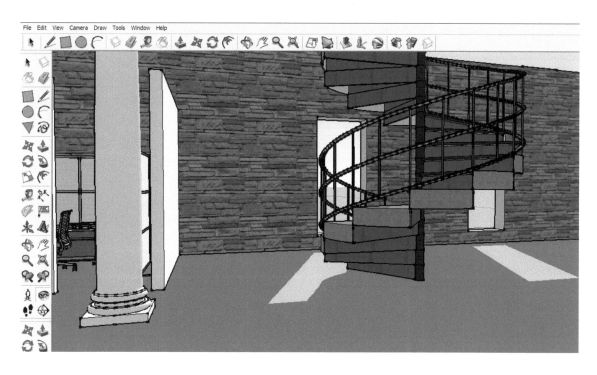

Figure 10.15

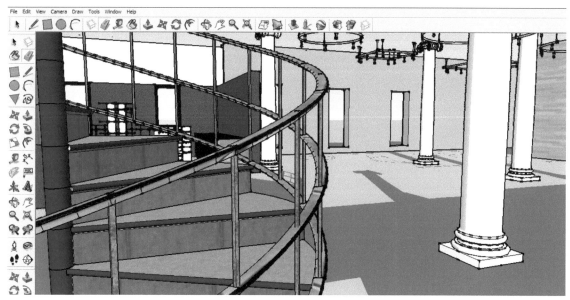

Figure 10.16

Figure 10.17

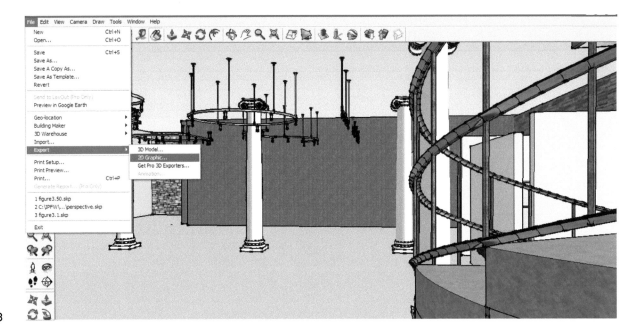

Figure 10.18

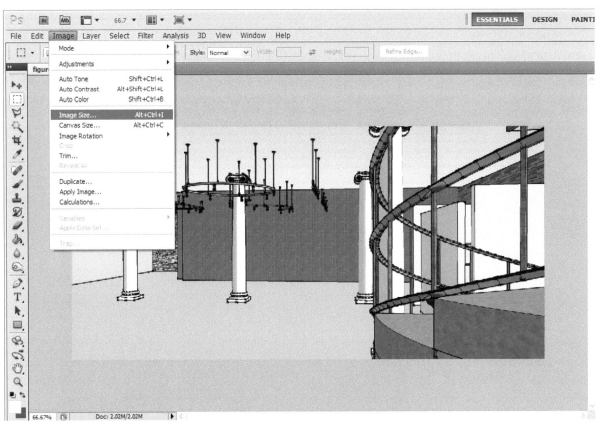

Figure 10.19

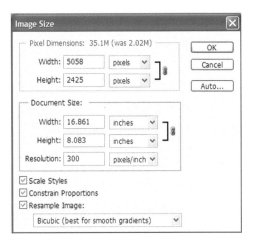

Figure 10.20

There are different ways to make a high-resolution file in Photoshop. One way is to open the file in Photoshop, select Image > **Image Size**, as shown in Figure 10.19. A dialogue box appears, as shown in Figure 10.20. Specify the **resolution** at 300 pixels/inch, as well as width and height as needed. You now have a high-resolution TIFF file that you can refine in Photoshop.

Saving AutoCAD Drawings to Photoshop

The line drawings, such as floor plans, elevations, and sections, can be created in AutoCAD. Then you can save the drawings to EPS format, which you can edit in Photoshop.

If you want to save a DWG file to a **PDF** file, select File > Print in AutoCAD. A dialogue box appears, as shown in Figure 10.21. Under Printer/Plotter, select the name as "Adobe PDF."

Specify the plot area by selecting what to plot. A dropdown menu appears, as shown in Figure 10.22. You can choose Extents, Window, or other options. You can also specify the scale.

Enhancing 3D AutoCAD Models in Photoshop

You can also import 3D models generated in 3D AutoCAD into Photoshop to enhance your models. The following is an example of a visual narrative that was composed in **InDesign** after 3D models had been enhanced in Photoshop. See Figure 10.23.

Visual Narrative: A Conversation with History in a Pantheon-Inspired Design

The Roman Pantheon is considered one of the great architectural marvels of history. Its massive dome combines art and science in a way that achieves a sense of both aspiration and mastery. Still, while the Pantheon as a science and technology feat has been undeniable for the 2,000 years of its existence, modernists bristle against such classical forms in their own work, preferring clean, bold lines and contemporary or futurist innovative thinking.

Some architectural works, such as the Crystal Palace, successfully straddle both worlds. These works contain classical references and awe-inspiring science and technology, yet also incredible innovation. The debate between traditional and modernist architects is an ongoing conversation.

The design proposed is a hybrid design solution that is inspired by the Pantheon in Rome yet brings in modern elements. It understands that architecture is a complete three-dimensional experience that goes beyond the façade and looks at the entire depth of experience—that is, it is a conversation with our past, our present, and our future, our history and our senses. This design will serve as a catalyst that stimulates the dialogue between modernists and classicists. Let the conversation with history begin!

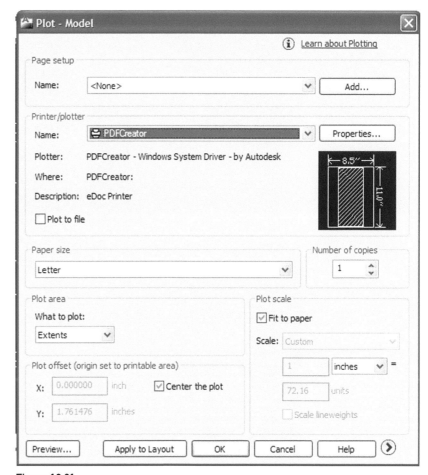

Figure 10.21

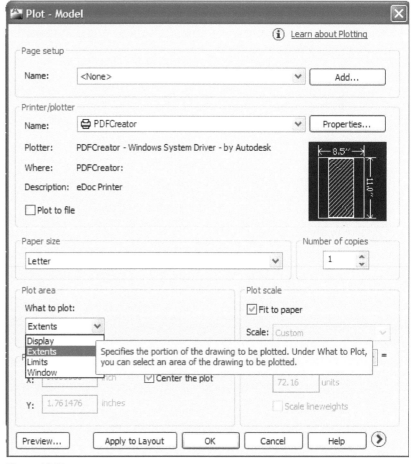

Figure 10.22

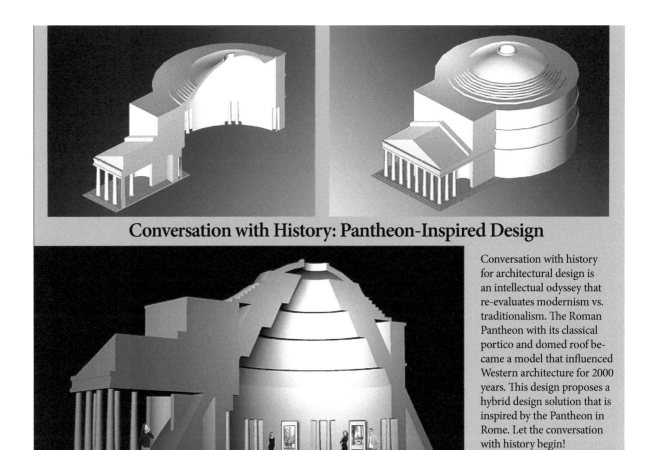

Conversation with History: Pantheon-Inspired Design

Conversation with history for architectural design is an intellectual odyssey that re-evaluates modernism vs. traditionalism. The Roman Pantheon with its classical portico and domed roof became a model that influenced Western architecture for 2000 years. This design proposes a hybrid design solution that is inspired by the Pantheon in Rome. Let the conversation with history begin!

Figure 10.23

Figure 10.24

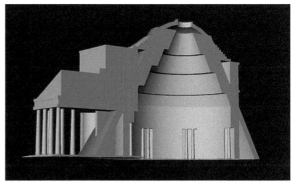

Figure 10.25

The following describes the procedure for creating this visual narrative.

1. Create a 3D model in 3D AutoCAD. Export the 3D model to .bmp files. (BMP, or bitmap, is a raster file format.) To export a high-resolution .bmp file, select View > Render > Advanced Render Setting. A dialogue box appears, as shown in Figure 10.24.
2. Export 3D models that you have created in 3D AutoCAD, as shown in Figures 10.25, 10.26, and 10.27. You can make the image resolution higher in Photoshop.
3. Open Figure 10.25 in Photoshop. Add lighting effect in the drawing as shown in Figure 10.28.

Figure 10.26

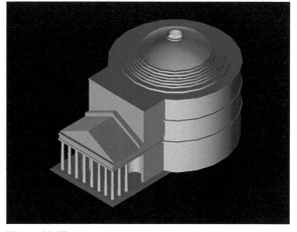

Figure 10.27

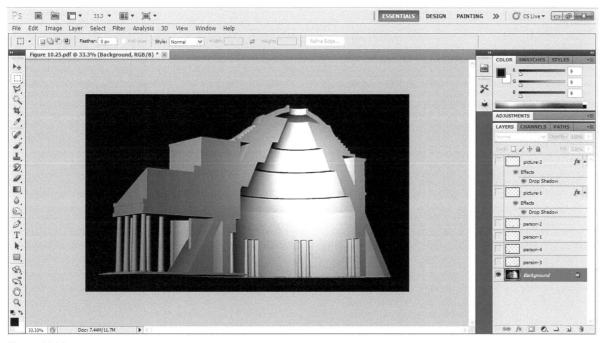

Figure 10.28

4. Add pictures on the wall, as well as drop shadows. You also can add human figures in the model in order to show scale. Make sure you put each object on one single layer. See Figure 10.29.

5. Open Figure 10.26 in Photoshop. Add lighting effect to the model. Then use the Gradient Fill tool to add the background as shown in Figures 10.30 and 10.31.

6. Open Figure 10.27 in Photoshop. Add lighting effects and use the Gradient Fill tool to add the background, as in the previous step. Your model should look like Figures 10.32 and 10.33.

Figure 10.29

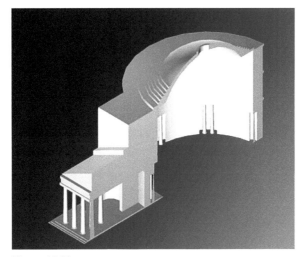

Figure 10.30

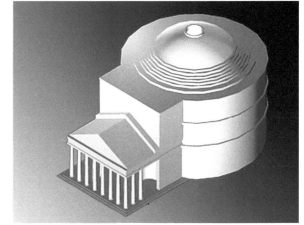

Figure 10.32

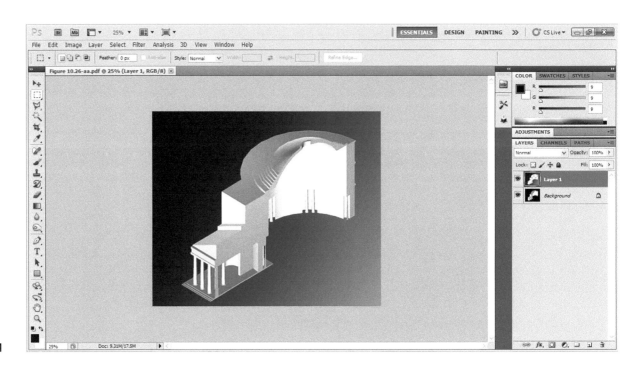

Figure 10.31

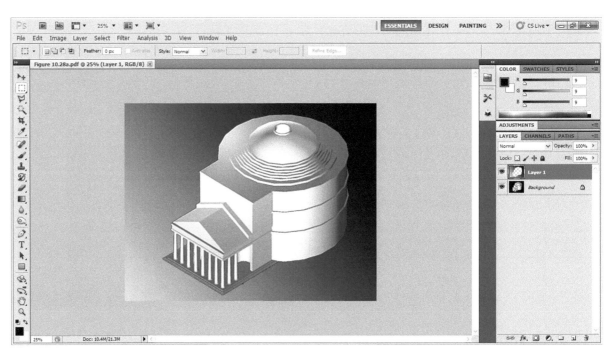

Figure 10.33